Whiskey is an expression of where you are. We try to interfere as little as possible with letting the grain or fruit express its essential nature. We add as much as is reasonable to the evolution of the whiskey, as an expression of New York State and of the Hudson Valley.

**Christopher Williams**
*Chief Distiller – Coppersea Distilling*

# Discovering The New York Craft Spirits Boom

## Heather D. Dolland

WALDORF PUBLISHING

Published by Waldorf Publishing

2140 Hall Johnson Road

#102-345

Grapevine, Texas 76051

www.WaldorfPublishing.com

**Discovering The New York Craft Spirits Boom**

ISBN: 9781634432610

Library of Congress Control Number: 2014958728

Copyright © 2015

# Dedication

To Amos, for your continued love, support and patience;
Because of you I was able to embark
upon the spirited journey of writing this book!

## Foreword by Julie C. Suarez,
### *Assistant Dean, Cornell University*

Walking the halls of the state capitol in 2007 with a small but committed group of farmers and food entrepreneurs, I never imagined that the creation of a new farm distillery license category would spark such tremendous growth. At the time, I was convinced this law would merely be a small change, enabling a few farmers the opportunity to grow crops for a niche market and opening doors for the next generation to start up their own distillery and add value to the home farm.

This book conclusively demonstrates the economic growth that can occur from positive public policy. I am impressed with the foresight of the author in showcasing New York's outstanding craft and farm based distilleries, and suspect a new edition will be needed in a few years time to accommodate new entrants. A thoughtful profile of each distillery, beautiful photographs and of course, excellent cocktail recipes make this book a treasure for local foodies.

# Table Of Contents

# HOW IT ALL BEGAN

I moved to New York from Grenada in August 1995, to study Architecture. Many times when I mention being from Grenada, I would be reminded of the U.S. intervention in 1983. It seemed to be the only point of recognition that resonated with anyone "over a certain age". Being 133 square miles with a population of 100,000, it is easy to understand why many would not be familiar with our presence in the Caribbean.

When I embarked upon the journey of writing this book, I had lived in New York for exactly half my life. Never would I have imagined in 1995 that in 2014, I would be writing a book about craft spirits in New York. But here we are.

I stumbled upon the realization of the vast number of craft distillers in New York State very much by chance. I was asked to help coordinate a food festival, when the thought occurred to me to seek local beer, wine, and spirit brands. Our objective was to promote local, so my thought was logical. What I discovered regarding the number of craft distillers in New York State was very surprising. For over eight years I was a Brand Ambassador responsible for promoting many national wine and spirit brands; yet I was completely unaware of all that happened that allowed all of these craft distillers to exist.

In the time it has taken to write this book, two more laws have passed, making this a very exciting time in the world of New York craft distillers.

Before writing this book, I never drank whiskey. What an initiation this journey has been. The title Discovering The New York Craft Spirits Boom was chosen very honestly. This experience has indeed been a revelation and discovery of my own preferences in the world of spirits, as I had the privilege of a tasting at every visit!

Meeting 30 distillers from Brooklyn to the Finger Lakes has created memories that I will never forget. They were all very gracious and generous with their time, for which I will remain eternally grateful. I spent two months discovering things that I previously knew nothing about.

What a time it has been. The hours spent sharing stories, and the art of distilling, allowed valuable insight into the world of a craft spirits distiller that I feel very privileged to now share.

Each chapter is dedicated to an individual distiller and tells his or her story regarding why they decided to embark upon this path. I met with some who were among the first in the business, and were instrumental in petitioning to get laws changed, as well as other distillers in their first year of operation.

During the time of writing this book, New York State is home to 55 craft distillers, with an additional 20 in different stages of the licensing process. At this rate, we are certainly poised to become the leading state for craft distillers.

For your enjoyment, I have also provided cocktail recipes, along with the locations where their products can be purchased and/or enjoyed. Their contact information has also been included, so in the event you decide to pay a visit, please let them know that Heather says "Hello!"

IN PHOTO: HEATHER DOLLAND & SOCA

# MY STORY

BRADLEY HAWKS (ASTORIA DISTILLING COMPANY)

In 2004, my friend, Kelly-Ann Ross-Daniel, also from Grenada, who owned a promotion agency in Brooklyn, needed someone to promote her brands on Long Island. At the time, I lived on Long Island and had a career as an Environmental Consultant. I have known Kelly-Ann since I was six years old, and she thought that my outgoing personality would be well suited to promoting her brands during my spare time. She was correct. I thoroughly enjoyed the experience, and not long after, began working with numerous agencies, promoting a number of national and international brands. What was supposed to be a favor to a friend ended up lasting nine years!

While visiting South Beach, Florida in October 2011, a shift occurred in my path while trying to decide where to have dinner. If you are at all familiar with South Beach--Ocean Drive to be exact--you are aware of the number of restaurants that line the street. Each restaurant has their assigned host or hostess whose job is to persuade you to dine.

One evening in particular, my mother and I were out to have dinner, and couldn't help but be enchanted by the beautiful dishes that displayed the evening's specials at each restaurant. It was impossible to choose a restaurant. I turned to my mother and said,

"Where is it written that we have to eat the entire meal at one restaurant? Why not enjoy each course where we will like to?"

Two months later, in the middle of a business lunch in Midtown Manhattan, the idea for All The Tastes of New York was born. It occurred to me to create a more formal dining experience, like the one that I had with my mother, and differentiate it from regular food tours by referring to it as a food crawl. This was achieved by making each restaurant course specific. Appetizer, entrée, and dessert is each enjoyed at restaurants that are a short walk from each other.

With the large culinary landscape that is New York City, taking the time to choose a restaurant can be very overwhelming. All The Tastes of New York eliminates this stress by providing restaurant and menu recommendations based upon the neighborhood that you would like to dine in. Our Food Crawls are all fully staffed events, providing exposure to the restaurants while creating a seamless experience for our diners.

As I started focusing on ways to build the company, I became interested in attending large-scale events that attracted hundreds, if not thousands, of people. Unfortunately, many were cost-prohibitive. I also realized that there were many other small businesses that faced the same challenges.

As I mulled it over, it occurred to me that with the relationships that All The Tastes of New York had with the restaurants, and the connections that I had with the countless brands that I promoted over the years, there was a database large enough to have our own Food and Wine/Spirits Festival.

With the success of each of our festivals, we saw the value of these events to brands that were still working on getting a foothold in the New York market. We were also introduced to more local beer, wine and spirit companies that we were not familiar with.

One such festival provided the basis of this book!

# THE INFLUX OF CRAFT SPIRIT DISTILLERS

The following is the general definition of a "Craft Distillery"

➻ the establishment must be independently owned

➻ the spirit must have been run through a still by a certified craft producer

➻ and produce no more than 100,000 gallons per year.

In 2002, state laws regulating distilling in New York began to change. From 2004 – 2007 Lobbying efforts by individuals such as Ralph Erenzo of Tuthilltown Spirits, Brian McKenzie from Finger Lakes Distilling, Derek Grout of Harvest Spirits, Jason Grizzanti from Warwick Winery & Distillery (Black Dirt Distillery), Bill Martin from Montezuma Winery (Hidden Marsh Distillery) and Julie Suarez, who was chief lobbyist for the New York Farm Bureau, resulted in the Farm Distillery Act which officially recognized distilling as a "Farm use".

The act also significantly reduced the size of the financial obligation necessary to obtain a distillers license. A three year Class A distiller's license (the "commercial" variety license) costs $50,800, which includes the license fee, filing costs and ancillary fees set by statute. A micro-distiller license was then made available for $1,450 for three years, as long as at least 75% of their raw materials were sourced from New York and production was kept under 35,000 gallons. In addition, the Farm Distillery license is issued on an annual basis with a total cost of $579.

The license also authorized sale in bulk from the licensed premises of the manufacturer as well as tasting rooms, to increase engagement with the public. Since that bill passed in 2007, 55 Farm Distilleries have started in New York State.

With these new regulations in place, the art of distilling that was forbidden since the days of Prohibition, now resulted in an avalanche of opportunities for local farmers and aspiring distillers alike.

While writing this book, on November 13th 2014, Governor Andrew Cuomo signed the Craft Beverage Act, amending certain provisions regarding manufacturing licenses, making it easier for craft beverages to increase their business. Tom Donohue – Special Counsel at the State Liquor Authority and Jacqueline Flug, the agency's General Counsel were instrumental in composing the law that the governor signed, along with Dennis Rosen, Chairman of the State Liquor Authority who was appointed with the mandate to address problems with the agency and led the efforts to gain passage of the bill.

The law provided the following:

➣ Allow each licensed manufacturer to conduct tastings and sell for on and off-premise consumption the alcoholic beverages it produces

➣ Allow each farm distiller to operate one "branch office"

➣ Change/ease the requirement for the on-premise license that a manufacturer can get

➣ Increase the production caps (without an increase in the license fee) for the "farm" and "micro" manufacturers as follows: farm wineries and farm cideries from 150,000 gallons to 250,000; farm brewers and micro-brewers from 60,000 barrels to 75,000 barrels; farm distillers and micro-distillers from 35,000 gallons to 75,000 gallons.

➣ Imposes minimum production requirements for licensed manufacturers: 50 gallons for any of the liquor, wine or cider manufacturers; and 50 barrels for any of the beer manufacturers.

What a different day it is. What was previously an illegal practice relegated to basements and nameless alleys has now made way for the dawn of a new day. Today, New York's New Distillers are feverishly making their mark on what it means to be "Distilled In New York".

Much like terroir; the geography, geology and climate of a region, is often used when referring to the effect that is has on the characteristics of grapes for wine; we are quickly approaching a time when we will refer to terroir in the making of spirits in New York as well. There has been a significant increase in the number of farmers of grain, to facilitate this new industry, giving the term "Product of New York" new meaning.

At the time of this writing, New York State has approximately 2,000 acres of malt barley. It has been estimated, that malt barley production will have to grow to 30,000 acres in the near future to meet the needs of New York State brewers and distillers. As a result, in January 2015, U.S. Senator Chuck Schumer launched an effort to establish

TUTHILLTOWN SPIRITS

a crop insurance program for malt barley to encourage further growth.

According to Senator Schumer, "Distilleries and breweries throughout the Capital Region pour local products and jobs into our economy, which is why it is important we continue to support this industry and provide them with the tools needed to succeed. In order for local craft distillers and brewers to expand right here in the Capital Region, we need a strong local malt barley industry, since the crop is so important to the production of beer and spirits."

Senator Schumer also noted that "the lack of insurance for malt barley is preventing farmers from planting this crucial crop. Without protections,

the risk is just too high, and that is preventing our craft breweries and distilleries from really taking off."

Senator Schumer urged the U.S. Department of Agriculture (USDA) to expand its malt barley crop insurance program to include New York State. He also called on the USDA and the federal Small Business Administration (SBA) to educate local malt barley farmers on federal financing. This is particularly important because it is anticipated that over the next decade, New York State will require farm craft brewers and distillers to source 90 percent of ingredients from local farms and malt houses.

This is certainly a great time to be drinking in New York!

# NEW YORK STATE DISTILLERS GUILD

The New York State Distillers Guild was formed with the realization that it is important for distillers to have a community. If they wanted to make legislative changes or even promote their presence in New York, having one voice is critically important.

In earlier years, when their numbers were significantly smaller, legislative changes and petitioning were very personal tasks. With their significant increase in numbers, the impact that craft distillers were having on the local economy could not be denied. Thus the existence of the Guild became even more valuable. Led by their current President, Nicole Austin, they act as the liaison between lawmakers and distillers as they help shape New York State laws that regulate the industry.

In addition to being the President of the New York State Distillers Guild, Nicole Austin is also the Master Blender at Kings County Distillery. Having studied as a chemical engineer, Nicole started her career as an environmental engineer, and realized that with her distillation knowledge, she could eventually have a career as a distiller. It was a

IN PHOTO: NICOLE AUSTIN

prospect that was particularly appealing.

As one who enjoyed drinking whiskey and found the history very intriguing, Nicole developed a desire to work in this field. However, when she graduated in 2006, there were not many opportunities available. With that realization, she began to actively pursue opportunities by attending any event that had 'whiskey' in the title.

When Nicole came across a blurb about Kings County Distillery's first event in a paper, she made a point of attending. She showed up, introduced herself, and let Colin Spoelman (one of their co-founders) know she would be working with them! At the time, there was no budget to pay her, but she wanted it so badly, she didn't care! Today, Nicole is a partner at the distillery. Since Kings County Distillery was the first distillery in NYC to get their license, it was a great union, as they also needed someone who had practical skill and technical knowledge.

# PEARLS OF WISDOM

There are approximately 70 distilleries at different stages of the licensing process. It occurred to me, that if this trend continues, there will be many who could learn from the wisdom of those who have paved the path that future distillers will walk on.

I sat with Ralph Erenzo, from Tuthilltown Spirits, in an attempt to harness and share some of the wisdom that he has gathered over the years.

When asked how he would advise people wanting to enter this business, given just how capital-intense this venture is and the many challenges and pitfalls, he couldn't stress enough just how critical reading and understanding the laws were.

Ralph said, "That is your template. It tells you everything that you can do. It is very specific. It does not tell you what you can't do. It only tells you what you can do. It is the opposite of any other American law. This only exists with alcohol laws, since they are so heavily regulated. If it does not tell you that you can do it, you can't."

"Regardless of what you want to do, if you want to innovate, that means that you have to ask permission. Then help a legislator understand what the innovation means, and how it will affect the industry and economy of the state. Not how practical it is. The law is the key to your operating plan."

The second thing would be to understand local zoning. Ralph went on to explain this to me.

"Get the local zoning manual. Consider your property. Sit with your local planning officer and fire chief, and get them to understand your vision. Establish those relationships face to face with your local officials, because they are all part of this."

Third, he told me, "Grow incrementally. Unless you have very deep pockets, do not go out and buy the best of everything. Grow into it. If you buy the best of everything, it will cost you considerably and you are locked into making something that has to sell. Remember there are no guarantees. After all is said and done, you still have to have a good product. People have to like it, and be willing to come back and buy it again. However, a lot of that has very little to do with the flavor, or the color of what is in the bottle. It has little to do with the shape or label. A lot of it has to do with the backstory. How did you get here? How are you telling the story to your consumers? Is it a story that they can relate to? Does it teach them a lesson? If it does, you will likely get them to come back and be repeat customers, because they are going to like you. They are going to like what you did. You are now creating a personal relationship."

Realizing that New York State includes many urban areas where a number of distilleries already exist, I asked Ralph about those who would like to see their dreams realized in such a setting. Where there is no opportunity to create an experience on acres of land, how he would advise such a person?

"One of the first things that you should look at is the history of the neighborhood that you want to be in. Choosing your site is critical. Find a site that has its own interest factor that you can interpret to the public as a story. Find a way to relate it to what you're doing. Make it relevant in some way to you by honoring the thing, person, or

event that happened there. Tell people about the event and how it affected people. How does your story affect them? It makes a difference."

His fourth point was to look at critical business factors. "Are you easy to get to? Can you be accessed easily using mass transportation? In a city, you absolutely need to focus on that. Interestingly, one of the benefits of an urban environment, unlike a more rural one, is from the standpoint of consumption. If your customers are using mass transit, there is not as much concern as those who have no choice but to drive. Be mindful of these elements."

"In general, you do not have to have a vision for where your business would end up, but have a direction in mind. Carve things out in the direction that you will like to go. Go out and sell your own product, be the face of the brand that the public knows. Develop a relationship with the stores and restaurant owners because you can rest assured that they have never met the maker of a larger brand. All of these things make a big difference."

# CATSKILL DISTILLING COMPANY

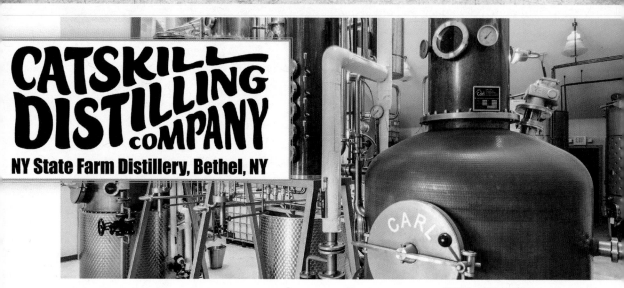

**CATSKILL DISTILLING COMPANY**
NY State Farm Distillery, Bethel, NY

PHOTO: JERRY COHEN

I was first introduced to the Catskill Distilling Company in the spring of 2014 as I was preparing for our Spring Cocktails and Eats event in midtown Manhattan. Several months later, in September, they were one of the local brands at our Astoria Restaurant Week Food Festival.

I can't say that I have ever had an inkling or desire to become a distiller; the thought actually never occurred to me. However, after meeting Dr. Monte Sachs, the idea began swirling in my mind. How absolutely enchanting the story he told of the world of distilling was. Though I can't say with certainty that it was his passion for his craft, or listening to the stories behind each product that had obviously been lovingly created, the seed was definitely planted!

With names like The Most Righteous Bourbon, Defiant Rye Whiskey, and Peace Vodka to name a few, the tastes and flavors are as ranging in length and breadth as the founder himself is skilled both as a veterinarian and distiller.

A native of Connecticut, Monte's first encounter with the art of distilling was during his veterinary studies in Italy at the University of Pisa. After making the acquaintance of winemakers skilled in the creation of grappa, and learning the art form necessary to produce an exceptional product, it turned out to be a pivotal point that rewrote the direction that his life would take. "It all began with Bernardini and grappa," he said.

When Monte made the decision to make whiskey, although he had an idea what was involved in the distillation process, he sought the tutelage of Lincoln Henderson, who was Brown-Forman's Master Distiller for forty years. Much like his experience learning the art of making grappa, his belief was, "If you want to learn, then learn from the best." A legend in his own right, with a career in consulting for some of the most well-known whiskey brands, Henderson agreed to teach him how to make whiskey. This was only after connecting over a stimulating phone conversation about chemistry!

Steps from the site of the 1969 Woodstock festival, the site of Catskill Distilling Company is also home to the Dancing Cat Saloon, which serves not only their own craft spirits, but craft beers and fine food. The tasting bar in the distillery also features an original bar from the World Fair of 1939.

His first product, Peace Vodka, is distinctive for its smoothness and delicate flavor. That was not at all the flavor profile that he was expecting when he embarked upon distilling it, but that was the way that it came out and he absolutely loved it. Peace Vodka is made with locally-grown red winter wheat and pure Catskill Mountain water. It is triple distilled, with no carbon filtration.

His second product, the Most Righteous Bourbon, was his collaboration with world-renowned distiller Lincoln Henderson. Lincoln Henderson taught him all that he knew about making bourbon. Having a teacher of such caliber resulted in a very superior product, one that he is very proud of. The Most Righteous Bourbon also secured a Gold Medal in the Fifty Best. His bourbon is aged for two years, and is distilled from corn, rye, and malt.

Curious Gin was the result of a month's worth of testing at least 12 to 15 different combinations of botanicals, in the quest of finding the perfect combination. Eventually, they settled on 14 regional and exotic botanicals and locally-grown juniper berries.

Grappa. I think it is safe to say that the love of this spirit has everything to do with the existence of Catskill Distilling Company. With a distillation process that was first codified by Jesuit monks around the year 1600, and used until the 20th century, grappa was created as a way to use materials that otherwise would have been wasted.

STACY COHEN.
IN PHOTO: MONTE SACHS, OWNER CATSKILL DISTILLING COMPANY

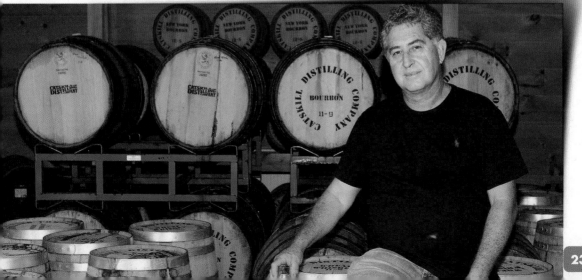

Their Bosco Monte Vecchio Grappa is a fragrant grape-based brandy, made by distilling pomace (skin, pulp and seeds) after pressing New York Riesling grapes grown in the Finger Lakes.

As Monte generally believes, it's not so much the raw product that determines what the end product will be, but who is distilling it. There are many variables. How is it being fermented? What yeast is being used? Who is the person behind the process? Because all things are not created equal, the character of the spirit reflects the character of the distiller.

One of the projects that he is very much looking forward to is his collaboration with Ommegang, a New York State Brewery. Using their spiced, unhopped Belgian-styled ale, distilling it and turning it into whiskey, they are currently waiting for this product to be ready to be presented to the public. It is currently aging 20 months with the intention of being released in late spring or early summer 2015. Although they are not certain of the name that this collaboration will bear, they are certain that it will be a fabulous product!

RESTAURANT

WOODSTOCK

DISTILLERY

## MAPLE OLD FASHIONED

2 ounces Most Righteous Bourbon
3/4 ounce Catskill Mountain Sugar House
1/2 ounce maple syrup
2 dashes of bitters

Muddle 1 slice lemon, 1 slice of orange w/ bitters and maple syrup. Add ice, pour 2 ounces of bourbon. Shake quickly. Top off with a splash of soda water, add cherry for garnish.

## VODKA NEW CUCUMBER

1 ounce Peace Vodka
1 slice of lime
2 ounces cucumber soda
Dash of creme de cassis ( for color)
2 slices of cucumber

Shake with ice and pour over fresh ice in a Collins glass and garnish with lemon.

**Catskill Distilling Company is located at 2037 Rte. 17B - Bethel, NY 12720**

### Locations where Catskill Distilling Company products can be enjoyed:

Mohonk Mountain House
1000 Mountain Rest Road, New Paltz, NY 12561

Flatiron Room
37 West 26th Street, New York, NY 10010

The Rivermarket
127 West Main Street, Tarrytown, NY 10591

### Locations where Catskill Distilling Company products can be purchased:

Astor Wine & Spirits
399 Lafayette Street (at East 4th St.), New York, NY 10003

Slope Cellars
436 7th Avenue, Brooklyn, NY 11215

Duke's Liquor Box
170 Franklin Street, Brooklyn, NY 11222

## BEES KNEES

1 ounce Curious Gin
3/4 ounce Catskill Mountain Sugar House Honey Syrup*
3/4 ounce fresh squeezed lemon juice

Shake all ingredients together and pour over fresh ice. Garnish with a lemon.

*Honey Syrup: Bring equal parts honey and water to a boil and let simmer until honey is dissolved in water (about 15 minutes).

# NEW YORK DISTILLING COMPANY

Tom Potter is no stranger to new ventures and walking the path less traveled. In 1987, he co-founded Brooklyn Brewery, when the idea of a brewery in Brooklyn was almost unfathomable. Serving as CEO and board chairman, in 2004 he retired from Brooklyn Brewery, and several years later began to consider starting another venture that would again allow him the opportunity to create a product. Excited to begin this new venture, this time with his son Bill Potter, he noticed the momentum that was beginning with craft spirits in New York. With this in mind, he began to research distilling.

As fate would have it, a mutual friend of Tom and Allen Katz asked for a meeting between the three of them, since he was aware of both Tom and Allen's desire to open a distillery. Allen Katz is the Director of Spirits Education & Mixology for Southern Wine & Spirits of New York, as well as the host of The Cocktail Hour, a weekly program on Martha Stewart's SiriusXM Satellite Radio. Allen and Tom decided to meet, and immediately realized that their specific skill sets would make for a great partnership. With that, New York Distilling Company was born.

Having a partner like Allen, who is

NEW YORK DISTILLING COMPANY

versed in the art of distilling, proved to be a great asset when they began to determine the products that they would make and what the flavor profile would be. Allen, who was especially fond of the idea of creating a Navy-strength gin, began to explore different flavor profiles that would be true to the styles they wanted to create, but also unique to them. They were also fortunate to have initial consulting advice from Jason Grizzanti and Jeremy Kidde, from Warwick Valley Winery & Distillery (Black Dirt Distillery is Warwick Valley's sister company), where they distilled their first spirits.

The New York Distilling Company's gins, Perry's Tot and Dorothy Parker, were developed simultaneously over a period of three to six months. In each case, Allen led the effort to achieve the flavor profile they both were seeking. In the case of Perry's Tot, their Navy-strength gin, the final part that allowed them to settle on their flavor profile, occurred when Allen experimented with honey as a botanical, which is not at all a traditional botanical. It had a wonderful result of bringing the flavors together; softening what may have been an otherwise "hot" gin, due to the high alcohol content.

Perry's Tot was named after Matthew Calbraith Perry, who served as Commandant of the Brooklyn Navy Yard from 1841-1843. Navy-Strength Gin is the historical proof that gunpowder will remain effective and can still be fired even if it were soaked by spirits. Perry's Tot is the first American interpretation of a Navy-strength gin, flavored with ingredients including grapefruit, star anise, cinnamon, and angelica root, and distilled with wildflower honey from upstate New York. This strength and style of gin historically has been synonymous with the British Royal Navy.

With the creation of their Dorothy Parker Gin, it was more a matter of getting subtle proportions right. Very small changes in the botanicals had fairly large impacts on the flavor profile. Balancing the floral nature of the hibiscus with citrus and other spices, then coming up with the right proportion for elderberry--which again, is not a traditional botanical--were all elements that needed to be worked out. This was necessary since these were their signature, unique botanicals. Dorothy Parker Gin is an American Gin, named after the famed poet, critic, writer, and enthusiastic drinker of gin. It embodies a blend of traditional and contemporary botanicals, including juniper, hibiscus, citrus, cinnamon, and elderberries.

Their Chief Gowanus New Netherland Gin is based on an American recipe dated from 1809. This was a recipe for making a version of "Dutch Style Gin" out of American rye whiskey. Dr. David Wondrich, who is widely hailed as the authority on the history of the cocktail, discovered this recipe in a book called The Practical Distiller, by Samuel McHarry. He came to Allen and Tom with the idea of recreating this recipe, which seemed right up their alley, because

the recipe called for a base spirit of rye whiskey. They were able to use their own un-aged, double-distilled rye whiskey which they re-distilled with juniper and Cluster Hops in the exact proportions suggested by the recipe. They also used hops that they believe were available two hundred years ago in consultation with Garrett Oliver, the brew master at Brooklyn Brewery and the author of The Oxford Companion to Beer. He suggested that Cluster Hops, a very old varietal that was grown in America in colonial times, was likely used when the recipe was first made. It was as close as they could get to this 1809 recipe. Allen and Tom created a reproduction of the original, which was meant to be a simulation of Dutch Gin of that time. Of course it wasn't, because they did not have the right ingredients; however, what they ended up creating was a new and unique American Gin that became common in the United States for fifty to one hundred years; a gin that had been completely forgotten, until they distilled it using that recipe.

One of the New York Distilling Company's newer products is Mr. Katz's Rock and Rye. Rock and Rye as a category of drink is a very old category. It was very popular in the United States in the late 1800s and from the early 1900s to World War II. Many bars and some people made their own. It is, by definition, a rye whiskey which is tempered with rock candy sugar. There is wide latitude to adding additional flavors to it. In their case, they infused a young rye that was typically between six months to one year old with rock candy and other organic sugar, and then infuse it with dried Bing cherries, cinnamon bark, and orange peel. They experimented with a number of ingredients, the more traditional ones included. What they ended up with was a fairly clean and simple recipe, with fewer ingredients rather than more. It was a recipe that had a balance of flavors, in which no single ingredient dominated, and this allowed their rye whiskey's ingredients--which they distilled from New York--to come through.

In addition to the distillery, New York Distilling Company also owns the adjoining bar, The Shanty, where cocktails can be enjoyed made with their superb spirits as well as other local and national brands. They are open seven days a week and it is a great place to visit and enjoy much of what Brooklyn has to offer.

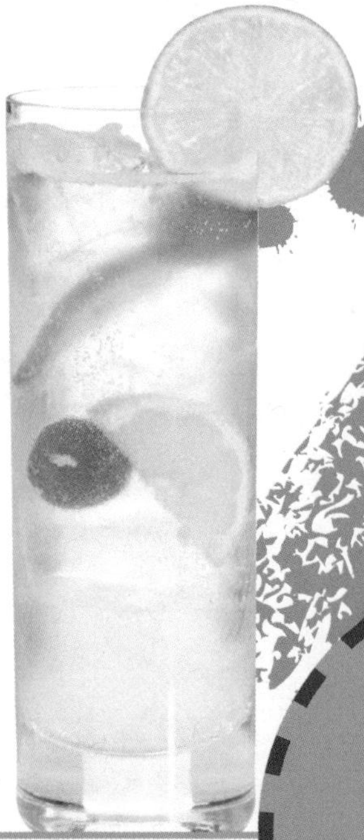

## RED HEADED STRANGER

1 1/2 ounces Dorothy Parker Gin
1/2 ounce blanco tequila
1/2 ounce lime juice
1/4 ounce grated ginger
1 cucumber slice
2 dashes Angostura Bitters

Mix ingredients and serve in a high-ball glass.

**New York Distilling Company is located at 79 Richardson Street (between Leonard & Lorimer), Brooklyn, NY 11222**

## CANNIBAL CORPSE REVIVER NO.2

1 1/2 ounces Perry's Tot Gin
1/2 ounce pear eau-de-vie
2 dashes Fernet Branca
1/2 ounce lemon juice
Splash of Prosecco

Mix ingredients and serve in a highball glass.

New York Distilling Company spirits can be purchased at the following locations:

Brooklyn Wine Exchange
138 Court Street, Brooklyn, NY 11201

Chelsea Wine Vault
75 9th Avenue, New York, NY 10011

Union Square Wine & Spirits
140 4th Avenue, New York, NY 10003

## STOMP & SWERVE

1 1/2 ounces Chief Gowanus
New-Netherland Gin
1/2 ounce Amaro Meletti
1/2 ounce Royal Combier
1 dash Dutch's Bitters
3/4 ounce lemon juice

Shake ingredients and serve in a highball glass. Serve with a grapefruit twist.

New York Distilling Company spirits can be enjoyed at the following locations:

The Shanty
79 Richardson Street, Brooklyn, NY 11222

Fort Defiance
365 Van Brunt Street, Brooklyn, NY 11231

Clover Club
210 Smith Street, Brooklyn, NY 11201

# ASTORIA DISTILLING COMPANY

I had the pleasure of meeting Chris Murillo, the founder of Astoria Distilling Company, when we were looking for local brands to be represented at our Astoria Restaurant Week Food Festival.

The journey that led Chris to create The Astoria Distilling Company began on New Year's Eve 2011, while celebrating with friends who were leaving to go to Puerto Rico to start a craft brewery. Although there are a number of craft brewers in New York, there are very few in Puerto Rico, and they wanted to be among the first.

QC

QUEENS COURAGE

Chris, who at the time was a practicing attorney, in addition to a cocktail & spirits enthusiast, was inspired to consider a similar venture. Craft distilleries were beginning to open locally, thanks in part to a recent change in New York State Law, but had not yet established a presence in Chris's home borough of Queens.

He started visiting as many distilleries as he could in Brooklyn and upstate New York, as well as Colorado, Washington, and Oregon. The more he looked into it, he saw opening a craft distillery as a great business opportunity. "The time was right, and no one else was doing this in Queens," he expressed.

As Chris began to do more research in order to determine the viability of the path that he wanted to pursue, he came across, the master distiller of Breckenridge Distilling who in addition to having a hard science background, also had one of the greatest palates that Chris had ever had the pleasure of working with, along with an artistic touch.

As Chris began to determine what he wanted to distill, a friend of his, suggested an Old Tom gin since there were not a lot of people making Old Tom gins.

Almost a third of classic cocktails from the pre-prohibition era called for this style of gin, and Chris realized this great tool could be available to high-end bartenders to create classic cocktails and impart authenticity that they have not had in decades. Queens Courage took shape as a modern interpretation of an Old Tom gin that is also a premium product.

BRADLEY HAWKS

In the 1600s, gin was first developed by the Dutch. At the time, they did not have the technology to make vodka, so they started with what was called a malt wine, now referred to as a single malt whiskey. The malt wine was then redistilled with botanicals. Due to the invention of the continuous still, most gins today start off as vodka. The vodka is then redistilled with botanicals to make gin.

Queens Courage is sweetened with honey, since it adds softness and flavor. Chris researched how to go about making Queens Courage, he wondered what it would be like to make his own malt wine and blend honey in it, taking inspiration from gin's origins in the 1600s. The result added a nice, round mouth feel similar to a whiskey, with a subtle sweetness from the malted barley. With the added sweetness, not as much honey was needed. It took a year and a half of going back and forth before he was able to settle on a formulation that he really liked.

One fateful day, as Chris was making sales calls on his bicycle, he saw someone in full beekeeping attire in the middle of Queens. He slammed on his brakes and said, "Dude, I need to talk with you, because I want to make gin from your honey!" They went to Chris's office, had some gin, and before long Queens Courage had a new supply of rooftop honey. The Brooklyn Grange has a farm located on the rooftop of the Standard Motor building in Queens, and supplies some of the honey for Queens Courage.

Another element that makes Queens Courage unique is the subtlety of juniper and pine notes, and the more prominent citrus component,

which is predominantly grapefruit. The grapefruit and honey add balance to each other. These bright citrus notes with a slight bitterness on the backend make Queens Courage a gin that can work well as a key ingredient in a wide variety of cocktails.

The goal of Astoria Distilling Company is to create spirits that are pulled from the cultural heritage of Queens. One such product in their pipeline is an ultra-premium version of Ouzo. Ouzo is the national drink of Greece, and since Astoria has one of the largest Greek communities outside of Greece, it is a natural progression. Doing a spirit that celebrates Astoria and its Greek heritage is very exciting since they are uniquely positioned to do so.

Chris is motivated by a desire to create experiences that bring people together, and that principle guides The Astoria Distilling Company in a quest to create high-end tools for bartenders (professional and amateur) to use as they do just that.

Chris believes, "The idea is not the business. It's all about the execution. Our product is and will continue to be superlative! Because the satisfaction you get from making something with your hands and putting into someone else's to try is extremely gratifying."

Cheers to that!

## LAVENDER COLLINS

(Compliments of Sal Milazzo)
1/2 ounce lavender syrup
1/2 ounce lemon juice
2 ounces Queens Courage
Splash of seltzer

Combine ingredients, except seltzer, in a Collins glass filled with ice. Shake and return to glass. Fill with seltzer and garnish with lemon peel (optional).

*Lavender Syrup: pour 1 cup hot simple syrup over 3 tablespoons of dried lavender. Steep for 12-16 hours and strain.

## TRIFORCE

(Compliments of Sal Milazzo)
3 ounces Queens Courage
1 ounce maraschino liqueur
1/2 ounce lemon juice
1 cucumber slice

Combine ingredients in a mixing vessel and stir with ice. Strain into a chilled cocktail glass. Garnish with a cucumber slice (optional).

### Queens Courage can be purchased at:

<u>Astoria Wine & Spirits</u>
3412 Broadway, Astoria, NY 11103

<u>Ambassador Wines & Spirits</u>
1020 2nd Avenue, New York, NY 10022

<u>Court Square Wine & Spirits</u>
2420 Jackson Avenue, Long Island City, NY 11101

### Queens Courage can be enjoyed at the following locations:

<u>Bowery Bay Bar</u>
1933 Ditmars Boulevard, Astoria, NY 11105

<u>The Sparrow</u>
2401 29th Street, Astoria, NY 11102

<u>Sweet Afton</u>
3009 34th Street, Astoria, NY 11103

## NORTH BEACH CUP

(Compliments of Sal Milazzo)
1 lemon wedge
1 dash simple syrup
1 slice of cucumber
1 1/2 ounces Queens Courage
1 ounce Pimm's
Splash of seltzer

Muddle lemon wedge and syrup in a Collins glass. Fill 3/4 with ice. Add cucumber, Queens Courage and Pimm's and shake vigorously. Fill with ice then add seltzer.

# KINGS COUNTY DISTILLERY

Kings County Distillery has the distinction of being Brooklyn's first modern-era distillery. Founded in 2010 by Colin Spoelman and David Haskell, their very distinctive whiskeys are made from New York grain, using masterfully-honed skills that connect Colin to his native Kentucky. In 2012, they moved their operation to the Paymaster Building in the historic Brooklyn Navy Yard, just steps from the legendary site of the Brooklyn Whiskey Wars of the 1860s and the former distillery district.

Their distillery is a model of sustainable and traditional whiskey production, using traditional copper whiskey stills fabricated in Scotland, and wooden fermenters built locally.

White whiskey. Although other cultures sell un-aged spirits next to aged spirits, in the United States, because of moonshine, white whiskey was never regarded highly by producers or distillers. They wanted to distinguish their product from moonshine, which had a bad reputation. When tequila was first introduced in the U.S. market in the 1960s, silver tequila didn't sell particularly well, because it was reminiscent of

moonshine. Realizing that the challenge was not as much due to the flavor, but rather the color, they invented gold tequila which is tequila with caramel color added; an obvious facet of marketing. Colin believes the reason that the craft movement exists as it does today is because craft distillers are trying to find the truth about what makes a spirit good.

Today his opinion of what makes bourbon good is considerably different from what he previously believed. As a person who started distilling at home, he learned a completely different set of variables that he realized made a significant difference. Good ingredients and more focus on the distillation process

# KINGS COUNTY DISTILLERY
## NEW YORK CITY'S OLDEST WHISKEY DISTILLERY

were key.

Kings County Distillery ages their products in smaller barrels, which enables them to have a full-flavored, mature spirit in a shorter period of time. By the end of 2015, they will be releasing a four-year-old whiskey--something that Colin is very much looking forward to. Nicole Austin, their master blender, has the task of determining each barrel's readiness and maturity.

When they began, since they were new to distilling, it took some time to figure out what the flavor profile was going to be. They thought that the grain and production would dictate the flavor, and it would be crafted in the distillation phase. They assumed that the flavor was almost set when it went into the barrels. Mashbill, yeast, and age were what they thought would be the main drivers dictating what their flavor profile was going to be. They just had to figure out the right time to take it out, and they would achieve consistency that way.

Of course, the thought process that consistent aging would lead to a consistent product was completely false, but at the time, they didn't know that.

"It's not like any of the big guys let you behind the curtains to see," Nicole said. "We don't ever get to see the barrels that do not make it into the bottle, so it was a lot of trial and error to realize how to craft Kings County's flavor."

To some extent, the barrels do tell you, and there were certain commonalities that Nicole would latch on to, to try figure out what it would be. In the beginning, she did not appreciate how important barrel blending was. When they opened up the first whiskey barrel and realized that no two tasted the same, they thought they had screwed up! Now they understand the nature of maturation; since the barrels do not come out of a lab, instead coming out of the ground, it is just the nature of a natural product. Consistency is something that is achieved by human intervention. It's a complex interaction that is hard to predict and even harder to control.

The flavor of their bourbon has not changed drastically since they started, but they are still trying to fight the perception that age is the determining factor of a whiskey being good. Colin hopes that in 10 years, people are not going to care that they are drinking younger whiskey because there will be so many craft producers that are making better younger whiskey.

Being able to communicate with their customers on a direct level is very important to their brand as a whole, rather than just reading text on a bottle. That idea of connectivity and being able to have access to the people making what you are drinking is very valuable. They want to encourage people to understand their values, to

see that they are using open fermentation, growing some grain on-site and using the pot stills, as a way to focus on understanding what the distiller goes through. It is part of their story and part of what makes their whiskey distinctive. Kings County Distillery's bourbon is not necessarily designed to be an improvement on Kentucky bourbon, but a distinctive, new kind of whiskey--excellent in its own right.

Having grown up in Kentucky, and being around moonshine-making, for Colin, that was part of the reason that Kings County Distillery exists today. Here is this thing that no one will admit knowing how to do, that was like a cultural secret so to speak. Colin found it very beguiling and intriguing. The only people who really knew how to do it carried the last name 'Beam'. There were three families that had apparent ownership over the knowledge of how to make whiskey. In America, opportunity should be open to all. The idea that whiskey could only be made by three or four families stopped being resonant. There was no reason that it couldn't be made in New York also. This is a world filled with misinformation and people feeling no confidence in their choices. But there was no need for Colin and David to feel overwhelmed by it. Trusting the integrity of a brand and knowing the people behind it has contributed significantly to Kings County's success.

Their plan is to grow the business very aggressively, because the only way to compete, not only in the national

**The distillery is open for tours and tastings every Saturday from 1 PM to 4 PM, and every Friday at 3 PM. Kings County Distillery is located in the Brooklyn Navy Yard, Building 121, 63 Flushing Avenue, Brooklyn, NY 11205**

marketplace, but also in the world marketplace is to have enough product. This is currently their biggest hurdle.

At the size their business is now, they are constantly running out of inventory. The ultimate goal for them is to have more people try the product and appreciate what makes Kings County Distillery different. However, more important than growth is the maintaining of their integrity. That is significantly more important to the business.

With regard to some of the new products that they plan to release, they have made a peated bourbon, and a brandy, the only non-whiskey that they have ever made. There is also a rye whiskey, oat whiskey, and single malt in the works. Moonshine, Bourbon and Chocolate are the three products that they currently have in distribution.

Of all of their products, their Chocolate Whiskey is becoming increasingly popular. They use Mast Brothers Chocolate, which has a factory close to Flushing Avenue in Brooklyn. A by-product of the chocolate making process is the husk. They are able to recycle it and pull flavors from it. The combination is essentially moonshine, plus ground-up chocolate husks.

Their brand does well in whiskey bars, as it is a unique product with a lot of flavor and character, very reflective of the founders themselves.

ALL THE TASTES OF NEW YORK

**Kings County Distillery products can be purchased at:**

**Astor Wine & Spirits**
399 Lafayette Street (at East 4th Street), New York, NY 10003

**Brooklyn Wine Exchange**
138 Court Street, Brooklyn, NY 11201

**Smith & Vine**
268 Smith Street, Brooklyn, NY 11231

**Kings County Distillery products can be enjoyed at:**

**Noorman's Kil**
609 Grand Street, Brooklyn, NY 11211

**The Flatiron Room**
37 West 26th Street, New York, NY 10010

**Brandy Library**
25 North Moore Street, New York, NY 10013

# GREENHOOK GINSMITHS

**S**teven DeAngelo started his career working on Wall Street as an interdealer broker. With the financial collapse in 2008, things began to change, and he started to reassess his career path. He began working on different business plans, and found distilling to be the most interesting, since gin was something he really loved and truly enjoyed.

"You never feel that this is something you could actually do or consider the possibility of making it yourself," Steven said. He began to notice what was happening over the last 10 years regarding the craft beers and guys making whiskey upstate (Tuthilltown), as well as people on the West Coast. Once he saw it as a viable business, he started working on a plan. It took him three years to get it up and running, and Greenhook Ginsmiths is the result of all of that planning. With no background in the

business and being completely self-taught, he went out to Arizona to learn how to use the equipment, because he realized how dangerous it could be if not used properly.

Although the Farm Distillery Act impacted the ease in which things could be done, the cost of running a distillery is extraordinarily expensive. With things to consider like zoning, permits, architecture, and plumbing, it is not an easy business to run. "Sales are not always what you think they will be and it is very capital-intense." Managing inventory, even with a product that is not aged for an extended period, creates a gap in cash flow.

Their American Dry Gin, which takes a year to age, is made from organic New York State-grown wheat, Tuscan juniper, coriander, chamomile, elderflower, citrus, Thai Blue Ginger, Ceylon cinnamon, Orris root, and elderberry.

Their Beach Plum Gin Liqueur is made from soaking whole Long Island Beach Plums in their signature American Dry Gin for seven months, with a touch of turbinado sugar.

Their third product, the Old Tom Gin, is crafted by over-proof bottling pot distilled corn, juniper, and botanicals inspired by the spice trade of a past time period. It was the prevalent style of gin in 18th-century England, and in their quest to recreate this historical, full-bodied product, they aged it for one year in bourbon casks before being finished in Oloroso Sherry casks.

Five to six years ago, there were no places available to go out and apprentice, so Steven had to figure it all out himself. From the beginning, Greenhook Ginsmiths has been dedicated to gin, and that is all they are interested in distilling. They currently have three gins and would like to focus on them primarily. Steven knows what he likes, so it was about finding tastes that are

GREENHOOK GINSMITHS

balanced. He is not fond of anise, so he couldn't have anise in his gin. All herbs, botanicals, and spices do not distill well, so it's about finding flavors that the distiller likes, that are balanced and work well together.

For his process, he uses a closed system because it is designed to work under a vacuum. A vacuum distillation process is a process that perfumeries used in the 19th century. It is a process that allows you to distill at really low temperatures, which is really helpful when distilling gin. Since raw herbs, spices, and botanicals are very susceptible to destruction by heat, this is a very desirable method. Using this process to distill at low temperatures, a lot of the herbs, spices and botanicals are protected, so the distiller can capture the botanicals as close to their uncooked flavors as possible. Given that heat both alters and destroys flavors, Greenhook Ginsmiths' process makes their gin unique.

**Greenhook Ginsmiths is located at 208 DuPont Street, Brooklyn, NY 11222**

Their American Gin took approximately 100 trials. With their Old Tom Gin, they were in product development since May 2012. You would think that because they know how to make gin, making another would be easier. That is completely not this case, since each style is different and recipes do not scale. Determining what would work and what doesn't is all trial and error. They make what they like.

Greenhook Ginsmiths is in 1500 locations, between bars, restaurants and stores in the Tri-State area. His clients are those who seek to educate themselves about craft spirits and take pride in drinking local. However, their sales are based upon the fact that, although they are a local brand, they carry a world-class product.

---

**Greenhook Ginsmiths' products can be enjoyed at the following locations:**

The Standard Hotel
848 Washington at 13th Street, New York, NY 10014

Jean-Georges
1 Central Park West, New York, NY 10023

Daniel
60 E 65th Street, New York, NY 10065

**Greenhook Ginsmiths' products can be purchased at the following locations:**

September Wines & Spirits
100 Stanton Street, New York, NY 10002

Soho Wines & Spirits
461 West Broadway, New York, NY 10012

Astor Wines & Spirits
399 Lafayette St., New York, NY 10003

## GREENHOOK AMERICANA

1 1/2 ounces Greenhook
American Dry Gin
1 ounce raspberry shrub
Champagne
Brandied raspberry for garnish
Lemon twist for garnish

In a flute, add above in-
gredients. Top with Cham-
pagne or sparkling wine,
garnish with a brandied
raspberry and a lemon
twist.

## MAYENNE FIZZ

1 ounce Greenhook Ginsmiths' Old
Tom Gin
1 ounce sweet vermouth
1 ounce Campari
1 ounce rose champagne
2 strawberries

Muddle one strawberry in
a mixing glass. Add Greenhook Ginsmiths' Old Tom
Gin, Campari and ver-
mouth. Stir with ice and
strain into a cocktail glass.
Top with Rose Champagne
and garnish with
strawberry slice.

## A SUIT OF SAILS

1 ounce Greenhook Ginsmiths'
Old Tom Gin
1/2 ounce Amontillado sherry
1/2 ounce St. Germain
Elderflower Liqueur
3/4 ounce fresh lime juice
1/4 ounce simple syrup
Lime wheel
1 kaffir leaf
1/2 serrano pepper de-seeded

Build in a highball glass.
Fill with crushed ice and
swizzle. Add lime wheel
and kaffir leaf. Top with
one ounce of club soda.

# PORT MORRIS DISTILLERY - PITORRO

Port Morris Distillery was launched in December 2013 by co-founders Rafael Barbosa and William Valentin.

Their flagship product, Pitorro, is also known as Puerto Rican Moonshine. Their story began after visiting family in Puerto Rico, when his uncle, Tio Rafael Rodriguez, kept making reference to the drink.

Tio Rafael was brought up in the town of Guayama, Puerto Rico, from where his recipe originated. Pitorro is the native drink of the island. It is customary that, when you visit someone's home, they offer you Pitorro. Although it is not legal, someone always knew someone who made it. Like moonshine was illegal in the United States, it is the same with Pitorro in Puerto Rico. Between November 1st and mid-January, there are constant check points to see if anyone is transporting the product, since it is illegal to produce.

Depending on where you live on the island, they may refer to it differently, but it is all derived from the same source. During his uncle's visit, he kept speaking about Pitorro, so Rafael decided to google New York City distilleries, and Breuckelen Distilling Company, Kings County and New York Distilling Company came up in his search. Raphael reached out

to Brad from Breuckelen, explaining what he was interested in doing, and Brad invited him to visit. Raphael was welcomed with open arms, and they explained to him the process of what was necessary to own a distillery.

They began to look for space in the Port Morris section of the Bronx, and were lucky enough to sell their business to a music producer, providing them with the capital necessary to start looking for a space. Rafael and William purchased a small still, placed it in the middle of the warehouse, and began to file for permits.

They also reached out to another distillery, Tirado, which was the first in

PORT MORRIS DISTILLERY

# PORT MORRIS DISTILLERY

the Bronx. Tirado shared information for his attorney, who helped guide them through the legalities of the process. "There has been a lot of comradery among the different local distilleries," Rafael said. He got his barrels from Breucklen Distilling. When they were ready to purchase a larger still, Tom Potter from New York Distilling Company invited them over and connected them to the company that he had purchased their still from. "The hospitality has been overwhelming," Raphael confided.

Although the culture in the Bronx is still a few years away from having the momentum that Brooklyn currently has, the Bronx community is very proud of Port Morris Distillery. They welcome as many businesses to be part of their community as are willing to participate. With The Bronx Brewery next door and Tirado Distillery one block away, Port Morris Distillery looks forward to becoming a vibrant hub for the neighborhood.

Since Raphael's uncle was a lifelong moonshiner, they are using one of his

recipes. When they first began, his uncle was their master distiller, but today they are all involved in the process of making Pitorro. The Shine is entirely his uncle's recipe and the Anejo (aged) they created together.

Pitorro is a very popular spirit for curing fruit. Add fruit to the Pitorro, put it in a jar, and place it somewhere dark for at least two months. After two to three months, the Pitorro will be fully infused. Using a variation of this method, they created their honey-habanero and tamarind-infused versions.

With their honey and habanero version, the Port Morris Distillery uses New York State products. The biggest brand is the Coquito, which will not be under the Pitorro label. It is made from coconut, Pitorro and cinnamon. Since they are not infusing the fruits like they did on the island, his uncle wanted to do an Anejo. They age it in brand new American oak barrels and in used whiskey barrels. Since this spirit does

not fall under the category of rum or whiskey, they applied for their own specialty label.

The Port Morris Distillery is currently working on the honey and habanero, which will both be launched in 2015. They make the habanero with the Shine and the honey with the Anejo. They ferment their product for 21 to 30 days and, after their mash becomes more like a beer or wine, they distill

**Port Morris Distillery is located at 780 East 133rd Street, Port Morris, NY 10454**

it. They also use a cooking yeast and not industry-standard yeast, in an effort to keep the product as natural as possible.

To date, the Port Morris Distillery self-distributes in New York as well as in local bars. Many of the liquor stores that carry their brand are in Manhattan and Brooklyn. They are going to be acquiring an additional 1400 square feet in the coming months.

**Pitorro can be purchased at the following locations:**

Manhattan Valley Wines & Spirits
984 Columbus Avenue, New York, NY 10025

Sterling Grapes & Grains
115 5th Avenue, Brooklyn, NY 11217

Riverdale Liquor & Wine
51 Riverdale Avenue, Yonkers, NY 10701

**Pitorro can be enjoyed at the following locations:**

Don Coqui
565 City Island Avenue, Bronx, NY 10464

Jake's Steakhouse
6031 Broadway, Bronx, NY 10471

Siete Ocho Siete
3363 E Tremont Avenue, Bronx, NY 10461

# NAHMIAS ET FILS - MAHIA

**NAHMIAS ET FILS**
**SINCE 1900**

**D**avid and Dorit Nahmia are the co-founders of Nahmias et Fils, in Yonkers New York. David came from a family that distilled Mahia, their flagship product in Morocco. The Jewish people were the only ones who produced Mahia, so when they left Morocco, there were few people who remained who knew how to make it. Those who did, produced it at home, and it was not the best quality. David had a dream to revive the practice of making Mahia, in the way that his parents and grandparents had made and sold it when he was a boy. No one produced Mahia in America and he wanted to introduce it as a premium product to the American market.

Although it was part of the tradition of Jewish people, it was consumed by all. The government made a lot of money from alcohol, even though they spoke about stopping it, but in the end, there was too much money to be made between the bars,

clubs and restaurants. It was very big business.

It was not at all uncommon for people to come to David's home asking for Mahia, so David was well aware of the goings on, even as a young boy. He had first-hand experience in the making and selling of Mahia as a business, especially during the holidays, festivities and parties when it was frequently consumed. In Morocco, Mahia means 'water of life'. (Ma – Water; Hia – of Life)

In New York, there are a number of restaurants that are interested in Mahia, as it is a new product that allows them to show an even wider range of creativity.

In addition to New York, Mahia has secured placement on a number of cocktail menus in Providence, Boston and Washington, D.C., in restaurants that serve a wide range of cuisines. With Providence being a big foodie

capital, Nahmia et Fils has experienced a lot of success in the local venues that focus on cocktails.

With many countries having products that are unique to them, much like tequila is to Mexico, David wanted to create a product that was native to Morocco. His desire is to make Mahia a household name.

Mahia is distilled from 100% figs, with no added sugar. Their entire process is from scratch. They get their figs from California, ferment it for two weeks, then distill.

Traditionally, Mahia is associated with having a lot of anise. The anise often overpowers the smell of the figs. When the Jewish people left Morocco and went to Israel, they made Arak, a product very high in sugar and anise, which everyone was used to.

With Nahmias et Fils' Mahia, the presence of anise is very minimal. They sought to allow more of the

flavor of the figs to come through. Theirs is over 50% alcohol with their particular still, allowing them to achieve a purer and better distilled product. They are also planning on making a different product out of dates. Because they do not add chemicals and just use figs, they source figs that will allow them to produce a consistent product.

The Mahia experience is a very unique one. It can be used in place of tequila for Margaritas and rum for Mojitos. Citrus largely brings out the flavor, and mixing Mahia with lemonade makes a very refreshing and great cocktail!

Another of their products is an un-aged Rye Whiskey called Leggs Diamond, after the famous bootlegger. Their Leggs Diamond is 100% rye, with no malted barley. They decided that in addition to making something as unfamiliar as Mahia, they should also create something that has a bit more recognition.

**Mahia and Leggs Diamond can be purchased from the following locations:**

Ambassador Wine & Spirits
1020 Second Avenue, New York, NY 10022

Park Ave Liquor Shop
292 Madison Avenue, New York, NY 10017

McCabes Wine & Spirits
1347 Third Avenue, New York, NY 10016

**Mahia and Leggs Diamond can be enjoyed at the following locations:**

Duo Bistro
50 John Street, Kingston, NY 12401

New World Home Cooking Company
1411 Route 212, Saugerties, NY 12477

Russell House Tavern
14 John F. Kennedy Street, Cambridge, MA 02138

## BLACK, WHITE & FIG

(Compliments of Kimberly Nagel)
The apples and figs become the sweet detail to a peppery base, and this cocktail is a great way to start your meal.
1/2 ounce Mahia
1/4 ounce simple syrup
Splash of lime or grapefruit juice
4 apple slices
5 cracks of pepper

**Combine apple, pepper, and simple syrup and muddle together in shaker. Add ice, Mahia and citrus. Shake and strain over ice garnish with apple slice in a black pepper & sugar-rimmed glass.**

**Nahmias et Fils is located at 201 Saw Mill River Rd, Yonkers, NY 10701**

## MAHINAMOSSA

(Compliments of Kimberly Nagel)
This ginger and chamomile iced tea is a wonderful way to finish the meal and relax.
2 ounces Mahia
4 ounces ginger & chamomile sweet tea
1/4 ounce fresh ginger

**Muddle ginger and tea in Collins glass. Add Mahia and fill with ice. Garnish with candied ginger.**

## NIGHT IN CASABLANCA

(Compliments of Kimberly Nagel)
A classic old fashioned, where fig martini meets bourbon... A great nightcap.
2 ounces Mahia
1/4 ounce bourbon
1 ounce dry vermouth
Peychauds or Angostura Bitters
1 sugar cube

**Combine ingredients in shaker, shake with ice and serve in a martini glass.**

# TUTHILLTOWN SPIRITS

The story of Tuthilltown Spirits began in 2001 when Ralph Erenzo, one of the co-founders, became interested in owning a rock-climbing ranch. The property in Gardiner was absolutely ideal for it. At the time, his son Gable, who was still in school in Colorado, transferred to SUNY New Paltz to be closer to home and to help with the ranch. This was a dream that never came to fruition.

As soon as he bought the property, which was originally 38 acres, Ralph began to face resistance from the neighbors, who were determined to stall him until he ran out of money. As the lengthy battle ensued, he began to sell parcels of property to pay lawyers, engineers, the mortgage, and to cover the expenses of day to day life. That battle lasted three years, and he did indeed run out of money. At that point, he began looking for something that he could do by right, and which needed no variance.

In 2003, Ralph contacted the local zoning officer to determine what he had the right to do with the property. They suggested a winery, since that is a farm use for which the area was already zoned. He started looking into it and familiarizing himself with the different laws. What he discovered was that, although a winery is a farm use, a distillery, which he was more interested in, was not at the time.

At around this time, he met his business partner and co-founder, Brian Lee, who was ready to get out of his corporate career and wanted to work with his hands. Brian wanted to buy the mill from him to make flour and corn meal. For 220 years, the Tuthilltown Gristmill, a national landmark, used waterpower to turn local grains to flour. However, after spending some time with the milling crew, Brian quickly changed his mind. They began to converse about Ralph's idea for the distillery. After a few days of consideration, they realized that they could secure the marketplace and accompanying media attention, since New York had not been known for having distillers since Prohibition. With that realization, they moved forward.

They found out that if they had a winery and applied for a distillery permit, they could make brandy from the wine produced. That would then make the distillery an accessory use to the farm. So they applied for the Farm Winery and A1 licenses at the same time. To fulfill the terms of their winery permit, they only had to make 50 gallons of wine per year, an achievable amount.

Not knowing much about each other or the business of distilling, Ralph and Brian's lives were suddenly and completely intertwined. Everything that they each had was on the line, since they funded the entire operation themselves. Brian designed and built the technical facilities and was responsible for engineering and all technical aspects of fermentation and distillation. Ralph was responsible for marketing and business development.

Soon after, another challenge arose, this time with the Department of Environmental Conservation, which sent along a letter stating that they would

TUTHILLTOWN SPIRITS IN PHOTO: CO-FOUNDERS RALPH ERENZO (LEFT) AND BRIAN LEE (RIGHT)

not be given any permits because their operation was considered an industrial use in the river corridor. Since they were next to a protected river and the New York Rivers Act did not permit for an industrial use within 500 feet, they were technically breaking the law. After much deliberation in Albany with the Department of Agriculture, they were able to prove that they were, in fact, a farm and their products were farm products, which allowed them to continue to operate.

Those were very challenging times. They were both financially extended and, unlike today, financing was not easy to come by. Brian ended up refinancing his house and they eventually sold The Grist Mill, the oldest continuously-operated water-powered flour mill in New York, and a house that was also on the property.

The tipping point for their business came in 2007 with the Farm Distillery Act. The impact wasn't as much financial as it was operational, since it provided them the opportunity to have

a shop and to take advantage of the tourism side of the industry.

When they started this business, because of the fact that the industry had not existed for eighty years, many of the things they needed to help their business did not exist. There was no manual. Any time they had a problem or a question for The State Liquor Authority, it would be the first time in four generations that anyone at the SLA had to answer such a question. Every-

TUTHILLTOWN SPIRITS

thing was new. No matter what they did, they had to change a law.

These days, things are very different at Tuthilltown Spirits. About three years ago, they were able to repurchase 12 acres, and are in the process of buying back the rest of the property, which will soon return them to the original 38 acres. The Grist Mill has since been converted to a restaurant, and the house will be a six-room Bed and Breakfast.

With the bed & breakfast, the restaurant & bar, the retail store and distillery, Tuthilltown Spirits is a very unique operation. Tuthilltown predated Gardiner. Named after Selah Tuttle, the site houses the old town hall and post office, and was a commercial hub before the current main street

existed.

Today, there are three generations of craft distillers in the United States. The first generation started in the late 80s and early 90s. The second generation were entrepreneurs, who wanted to change the post prohibition laws and make it more feasible to have a small craft distillery. The third generation emerged due to an increase of friendly laws that allowed a tremendous influx to occur.

Joel Elder Tuthilltown's Chief Distiller and R&D alchemist is responsible for creating Tuthilltown's new product lines. He developed their Half Moon gin and the first variant, Half Orchard. He is looking not only at botanicals and citrus, but base spirits as well. Whereas a lot of gins

start with neutral grain spirit, his task is to start with a well-created, delicious base spirit, distilled from apples and wheat, and then choose the botanicals that would best compliment it.

To date, there are six whiskies, one gin, two vodkas, cassis, cocao and bitters. With 12 products on the shelf and 13 products in research and development, the business has certainly entered into a very desirable stage of production. By 2015 there will be at least 25 products in their tasting room all made by them, and 15 on the market. Quite an accomplishment for a company that had such a "rocky" start!

Tours are available every weekend, year-round, and can be scheduled by visiting http://www.tuthilltown.com

**All Tuthilltown Spirits products are available for sale at their Distillery Shop at Tuthilltown Spirits, 14 Grist Mill Lane, Gardiner, NY 12525, as well as at their online store http://store.tuthilltown.com**

### Tuthilltown Spirits can be purchased at the following locations:

Astor Wine & Spirits
399 Lafayette Street, (at East 4th St.), New York, NY 10003

Whiskey & Wine off 69
1321 2nd Avenue, New York, NY 10021

Union Square Wine & Spirits
140 4th Avenue, New York, NY 10003

### Tuthilltown Spirits can be enjoyed at the following locations:

Clover Club
210 Smith Street, Brooklyn, NY 11201

Flatiron Room
37 West 26th Street, New York, NY 10010

Jean-Georges
1 Central Park West, New York, NY 10023

## EVENTIDE COCKTAIL

(Compliments of Warren Bobrow.
Please check out his cocktail book, Apothecary Cocktails)
2 ounces Hudson Baby Bourbon
1/2 ounce Fruitations Cranberry Soda and Cocktail Syrup
1 ounce Perrier Sparkling Mineral Water (lemon)
3 dashes Fee Brothers Whiskey Barrel Bitters
Hand-cut ice in huge cubes

**In a Boston shaker, add the Baby Bourbon and the Fruitations Cocktail syrup. In the other side add the ice, shake hard for 15 seconds. Strain into an Old Fashioned glass over a large ice cube. Add the Perrier Sparkling water, three dashes of Fee Bros Bitters over the top and sip.**

## WHISKEY MILKSHAKE

(Compliments of Rebecca Bills, executive pastry chef at Holsteins Shakes and Buns in Las Vegas, NV)
4 large scoops vanilla ice cream
4 tablespoons strawberry jelly
1 ounce Hudson Manhattan Rye
4 tablespoons blueberry jam
Whipped cream, for garnish
1 tablespoon freeze-dried blueberries, for garnish
1 tablespoon freeze-dried strawberries, for garnish

Take ice cream out of the freezer to soften. In the meantime, stir the straw-berry jelly in a small bowl until smooth and transfer to a small squeeze bottle or piping bag with a plain tip. Swirl the strawberry jelly onto the inside bottom of your milkshake glass. Place ice cream, rye, and blue-berry jam in a blender and blend until smooth.

Pour the blended shake into milkshake glass. Gar-nish milkshake with a swirl of whipped cream and top with a sprinkling of freeze-dried blueberries and strawberries.

## FARMER'S DAUGHTER
### (COMPLIMENTS OF STUART JENSEN)

1 1/2 ounces Carpano Bianco
1/2 ounce Half Moon Orchard Gin
3 snap peas
4 pieces kumquats
1/2 ounce lemon juice
2 ounces Fever Tree Tonic

Muddle the kumquats and snap peas in a shaker tin. Add the gin, vermouth and lemon juice and shake with cold draft ice. Strain into a Collins glass with cracked ice and top with tonic water.

# DENNING'S POINT DISTILLERY

Karl and Susan Johnson are the founders of Denning's Point Distillery, founded in 2014 in Beacon, New York. Karl grew up on a 6000-acre farm in Minnesota. His father was a plant geneticist, and he wrote his thesis on malting barley for beer, a subject that had interested him for many years. Later in his career, he distilled rocket fuel components, and never forgot the experience and how much he loved it. Being fascinated with distilling, the idea of becoming a distiller was not far-fetched, and was very appealing to Karl.

As Susan and Karl visited local liquor stores, they began to notice an increase in products from local distillers. They began to look into the changes that occurred to make it all possible for these distillers to exist.

With Susan's background in marketing, they thought their skillsets would make for an ideal partnership. She would take care of product development and direction, and Karl would focus on distilling, operations, and equipment.

Their first spirit, which is their flagship product, is Beacon Premium Reserve American Whiskey. With a nose of vanilla, caramel, and a long butterscotch finish, it is distilled from 100% corn mash. For this product, they do the barrel selection and all of the blending.

Their Viskill Vodka is distilled from New York State winter wheat. Distilled one time and filtered continuously for three days with carbonized coconut shells, this spirit offers a unique complexity. Their Viskill Vodka takes its name from the original Dutch word for the Fishkill, a creek that meanders for 33 miles through the Hudson Valley. It was this creek that provided a safe

haven for the Continental soldiers during the Revolutionary War, who would camp there. Denning's Point Distillery has included the blue sash on their Viskill Vodka bottle, inspired by the blue sash worn by the commanding generals to differentiate themselves from the foot soldiers. They also included Benjamin Franklin's famous "Join or Die" snake symbol, created in an effort on Franklin's part to convince the colonies to join together against the British. It is divided into thirteen segments, representing the original colonies. The history all comes together to tie their brand to the area.

Their Denning's White Rye Whiskey is aged for five days in a whiskey barrel.

ALL THE TASTES OF NEW YORK

This unique, raw, rye spirit has hints of fruit wood on the nose and spice on the palette. It is a complex and sophisticated interpretation of traditional moonshine.

Denning's Point Distillery is currently operating out of a converted garage. Having all of the utility components for everything that they needed, like floor drains, the space was a great find. What used to be the office for the previous business has been converted into their tasting room, being that it is a very light and airy space.

At the time of our interview, they had only been open for eight weeks. As Susan recalled, when she went to file for their permits, there were 55 distilleries in New York State. That number has since grown to 70.

Karl and Susan base everything they create according to their own taste. They are currently working with someone who forages for wild herbs in the Hudson Valley, and are planning on doing a wild herb-infused spirit. With such a young business, there are a number of details that are still being worked out, including the right shade of blue to represent their brand.

Denning's Point Distillery is the perfect marriage of an urban distillery and farm distillery, located in the agricultural part of the state, in an urban setting.

Denning's Point Distillery is located at 10 North Chestnut Street, Beacon, NY 12508

**Denning's Point Distillery products can be purchased from the following locations:**

<u>Arlington Wine & Liquor</u>
Arlington Square, 718 Dutchess Turnpike, Poughkeepsie, NY 12603

<u>Viscount Wines & Liquors</u>
1173 U.S. 9 Wappingers Falls, NY 12590

<u>Ambassador Wine & Spirits</u>
1020 2nd Avenue, New York, NY10022

**Denning's Point Distillery products can be enjoyed at the following locations:**

<u>Max's on Main</u>
246 Main Street, Beacon, NY 12508

<u>Roundhouse</u>
2 East Main Street, Beacon, NY 12508

<u>Dogwood Cafe</u>
East 47 Main Street, Beacon, NY 12508

# ADIRONDACK DISTILLING COMPANY

In December 2010, Bruce Elwell, Jordan Karp, and Steve Cox met for breakfast to discuss the possibility of going into business together. Having a mutual love of spirits, specifically vodka, they wanted to create a product that used local ingredients, free of additives, and that was gluten free.

In 2011, Adirondack Distilling Company was formed. Bruce is the President and CEO and handles most of the business development. His partner, Jordan, does most of the formulation, connects with the government agencies, and focuses on research and development. Bruce's wife, Anita Elwell, takes care of the day to day business management part of the operation. Steve has since moved on to another endeavor.

With degrees in microbiology, biology, bio-chemistry, and business administration, Bruce saw the opportunity to become a distiller as an extension of chemistry. He always had the desire to own a winery, since he very much enjoys wine, so when the idea was presented to him to own a distillery, it was not far removed.

Jordan grew up on Long Island, and was involved with politics for 10 years before he was sent to upstate New York in 2006 to run a campaign. He enjoyed living there and wanted to find a way to move back. While he was living in Washington, D.C., he saw an email about small distilleries opening in New York, and decided to text his friend Steve about how to make alcohol. After that conversation, it seemed like a plausible idea worth exploring.

The Farm Distillery Act lowered many

ALL THE TASTES OF NEW YORK

of those barriers. Being able to have their own tasting room and being able to directly connect with their consumer was a game changer. It made it easier for the smaller guys to compete with the big brands. In the wake of the financial crisis, more people really examined where they are spending their money and they are doing a lot of voting with their wallets. Consumers want quality, locally produced products. The buy local movement is huge.

After their breakfast meeting in December 2010, Bruce, Jordan, and Steve decided the idea of opening a distillery was worth exploring, and they began working on a business plan. They took their business plan to the bank and got a loan, thereby committing to living with whatever the possible outcome of their endeavor might be.

In a business that is so capital-intense, a joke among small distillers is that the two things you don't have enough of in preparing for this business are floor drains and money.

One of the great things about New York State distillers is that they are very open. When the Adirondack Distilling Company began, they reached out to Harvest Spirits, Tuthilltown, and a number of other distillers who were very helpful in giving them the guidance they needed. "We are all small fish, but together, we can make a big impact," Jordan said. The other

distillers were a great source of information and knowledge. As Jordan pointed out, it is that comradery that "speaks to the spirit of the Farm Distillery Act. We are not so much competing with each other as we are competing against the big brands." These distilling companies have a unique philosophy of being in it together, even though they are separate companies.

There is nothing like getting your own

ADIRONDACK DISTILLING COMPANY

equipment and turning the still on for the first time. Their first distilled spirit was their ADK Vodka. Their ADK Gin came about nine months later. A lot of research and development went into the gin. The gin was Bruce's baby. He knew what he wanted with regard to taste, so he searched for something that made their gin unique and memorable. Aside from being one of only two corn-based gins in the world, as far as he is aware, Bruce discovered and engaged the unique taste of the Alpine Bilberries. Alpine Bilberries are indigenous to the Adirondacks, so he started playing with his exclusive recipe in a London Dry Style Gin. He brought batch #1 to the distillery, and realized they had discovered the foundation of what they wanted their gin to taste like. It took them over a year to settle on what they thought best represented their one-of-a-kind ADK Gin. They also found that the way they rest the spirit before they proof it and bottle it allows some of the flavors to develop on their own. By letting the gin rest and meld on its own, the flavor profile is much more robust. It is one of the things that contribute to making their product unique. Distilled with 10 botanicals and essentials oils, the Alpine Bilberries gives their ADK Gin a smooth and aromatic flavor.

Their ADK Vodka is crafted from 100% New York State corn and is chill-filtered over Herkimer diamonds for about six hours. Their ADK Gin is one of a handful of gluten-free gins in existence. They also make an award-winning white whiskey called 1,000 Stills White Whiskey. It is produced from local corn, which is also chill-filtered and made with water from the Adirondacks. The Adirondack Distilling Company makes all of their own alcohol, and does not bring in any outside spirits. They very much pride themselves on making their own neutral grain product.

Their bourbon is also 100% corn, unlike most that are 51%. They are working on a single-malt and have a barrel-aged gin that is currently awaiting federal and state approval. Old Oak Gin should be on the market in early 2015.

The Adirondack Mountains' water in upstate New York plays a huge role in the flavor profile of their spirits as well.

Adirondack Distilling Company's entire line is naturally gluten-free since corn is gluten-free. In two years, their products have won 10 awards, most in international competitions, and several in New York State. Their ADK Vodka is the winningest. It has won seven-awards, including a world competition in London, where it took Silver in the World Vodka Awards. Several local bars and restaurants carry the Adirondack Mountain Distillery brand, and it can be seen on several cocktail menus.

Adirondack Distilling Company is located at 601 Varick Street, Utica, NY 13502

## ADIRONDACK CIDER

2 ounces 1000 Stills White Whiskey
2 ounces apple cider
1 ounce brown sugar simple syrup
1/2 ounce lemon juice

**Combine over ice and stir.**

Adirondack Distilling Company products can be purchased at the following locations:

Ambassador Wine & Spirits
1020 2nd Avenue, New York, NY 10022

Union Square Wine & Spirits
140 4th Avenue, New York, NY 10003

Park Slope Liquors
158 Park Place, Brooklyn, NY 11217

Adirondack Distilling Company products can be enjoyed at the following locations:

Brooklyn Social
335 Smith Street, Brooklyn, NY 11231

Saxon & Parole
316 Bowery, New York, NY 10012

Mae Mae café
68 Vandam Street, New York, NY 10013

## 601 PUNCH

2 ounces 601 Bourbon
2 ouncesblood orange soda
2 ounces grapefruit juice
2 ounces sparkling cherry juice
1 ounce rosemary simple syrup

**Combine in tumbler over ice, garnish with citrus.**

## ADK GIN COLLINS

2 ounces Adirondack ADK Gin
2 ounces fresh lemon juice
1 ounce simple syrup
6-8 fresh blueberries
2 ounces club soda

**Muddle blueberries with simple syrup, build over ice and rest of ingredients.**

# PROHIBITION DISTILLERY

**B**rian Facquet always wanted to be a microbrewer. While working in corporate America in New York City, he met his partner John Walsh, an old friend and his HR Director on the crosstown bus one morning. They both worked for the same company, and both John and Brian wanted to start a craft brand.

When Brian came out of the Navy, he had the opportunity to invest in Blue Point Brewing on Long Island. He had passed on that opportunity, based upon his father's advice. Fifteen years later,

ALL THE TASTES OF NEW YORK

Prohibition Distillery was created. His father was one of their first investors.

Born in New Orleans and raised on Long Island, Brian currently lives in Hoboken, NJ. Although Brian does not come from a family of distillers, the trade has touched his family over the years. In the 1920s, his family made illegal liquor in New Orleans, as many did in those days. In the late 1800s, his great-great-grandfather on his mother's side, a railroad engineer, followed the rum trade from New Jersey to Cuba. His great-grandfather then followed the rum trade back to New Orleans, met his wife and brought her to Cuba. When he returned stateside, he ended up as the engineer of the Southern Pacific Railroad in the early 1900s.

Prohibition Distillery was founded in 2008. In 2009, they started sharing space at Tuthilltown Spirits. During that time, the distillation business in New York was in its infancy and sharing space seemed like a good solution, especially since they did not have the experience or the capital to acquire their own.

Their first spirit was Bootlegger 21 New York Vodka. They didn't know how to make vodka, but they did know that they wanted something that was clean. In February 2010, their first four bottles of Bootlegger 21 Vodka were sent to the San Francisco International Spirits Competition and won Silver. In late 2010, after figuring out how to scale up production (beyond a few bottles), they launched. They submitted it and won Best Vodka and the only Gold Medal at the New York International Spirits Competition in their first week on the market. They put it in to get feedback, and ended up beating many major brands! They have since won several more Golds. Recently they won a double Gold at 50 Best American Competition, and were named by Travel and Leisure as one of the top vodkas in the world. They were the only one from the United States. They have been making their Bootlegger 21 Vodka now for five years. They filter their vodka slowly through charcoal, with the result being very smooth, yet having subtle character.

ALL THE TASTES OF NEW YORK

In 2013, Prohibition Distillery opened its own space in a small firehouse in Roscoe, NY. They immediately began production of bourbon and started formulating gin. All of their products are made from 100% corn and are certified Kosher by the Orthodox Union.

Their Bootlegger 21 New York Gin is made using the old technique of steeping, called maceration, which is how the old London Dry gins were made. Their inspiration was from the classics Beefeater, Tanqueray & Plymouth, which used very few ingredients to extract the tastes that have defined their category. They had no desire to redefine gin, but they did want to use similar botanicals to create an update without using citrus. This would be their modern take on an original London Dry. They use juniper berries, coriander, lemon verbena, orris root, and bitter orange as their botanicals.

The process of creating Bootlegger 21 Gin was certainly unlike many given Brian's method of execution for the first batch. After spending a year test-distilling small batches, they were ready for the big batch in their 300-gallon pot still. Due to the illness of Brian's partner, John, and a scheduled trip to Tales of the Cocktail, Brian was caught in a crunch for time. The intimate understanding of the elements of each ingredient in the gin, and how they changed over time, made considerable difference as they scaled up. With the help of his assistant distiller, Kyle DeCotes, they would add a certain number of pounds of each ingredient daily, which Brian would taste and then add to as he went along. The result is like jazz...each ingredient playing its own note, yet coming together to make a beautiful spirit.

Their Bootlegger 21 New York Bourbon is made from 100% corn, distilled to 143-proof and then barreled at 119-proof in new charred oak barrels. They use various sized barrels, as the shortage of barrels makes it hard to depend on suppliers. The first releases have been aged in five-gallon barrels for over 12 months. Flavors of cinnamon, Red Hot candies, vanilla, and oak linger on the pallet of this unfiltered 92-proof bourbon. With regard to creating the flavor profile for their bourbon, they paid very close attention to their heads and tails cuts, and let the spirit guide them. Brian says that if he doesn't know the answer or runs into trouble, he picks up the phone and calls another distiller or a consultant that they work with. At this point, with the number of distilleries that exist, he would often contact any number of them, since he has friendships with many and they all share knowledge.

Brian acknowledges that as a New York State distiller, he has no desire to be compared to other local distillers, since they are a group of peers. "Everyone brings something different to the table. We are all figuring it out." Their focus is on creating a great product and their goal is to rebuild a town one drink at a time.

**Prohibition Distillery is located at 10 Union Street, Roscoe, NY 12776**

## C'EST VOTRE MONDE

(Compliments of Robert Mack at
The Speakeasy in Albany, NY)
1 1/2 ounces Bootlegger Gin
1/2 ounce St. Germain
1/4 ounce maraschino liqueur
1/2 ounce lime juice
1 brandied cherry

**Shake, pour in coup glass.
Garnish with a brandied
cherry.**

## THE BOOTLEGGER "BOULEVARDIER"

(Compliments of Robert Mack at
The Speakeasy in Albany, NY)
1 1/2 ounces Bootlegger Bourbon
3/4 ounce Carpano Antica
3/4 ounce Cappelletti
Orange zest

**Stir in rocks glass. Garnish
with orange zest.**

## THE NEW YORK MINUTE

(Compliments of Robert Mack at
The Speakeasy in Albany, NY)
1 1/2 ounces Bootlegger Vodka
1/2 ounceclover honey syrup
4 ounces sage infused lemonade
Sage-infused lemon wheel

**Build in a highball glass
and garnish with a sage-infused lemon wheel.**

**Prohibition Distillery products
can be purchased through the
following distributors:**

Empire Merchants South
16 Bridgewater Street, Brooklyn,
NY 11222

R & R Marketing
10 Patton Drive, West Caldwell,
NJ 07006

Horizon Beverages
80 Stockwell Drive, Avon,
MA 02322

**Adirondack Distilling Company
products can be enjoyed at the
following locations:**

Rainbow Room
30 Rockefeller Plaza, New York, NY
10112

Nick & Toni's Café
100 West 67th Street, New York, NY
10023

Nobu
105 Hudson Street, New York, NY
10013

# FINGER LAKES DISTILLING

**B**rian McKenzie is very much at home in the Finger Lakes, being born and raised there. When he got married, both he and his wife, Jennifer, knew that was where they wanted to live, since she is also from the area.

Brian knew he wanted to transition out of finance, and he began to contemplate what he wanted to do with his life. He considered doing something that would be associated with the wine trail, since it is a booming industry, with millions of people visiting to sample the wines each year.

Although he liked wines, he enjoyed whiskey more, and Brian and Jennifer thought the Finger Lakes would be a good location for a distillery. They knew from the beginning that they would

ALL THE TASTES OF NEW YORK

differentiate themselves by being a spirit producer; not just whiskey, but also gins and vodkas. His passion, however, was whiskey.

In 2007, as he started to work on their concept, he realized early on that the type of business they wanted to open wasn't allowed in New York State. They wanted the opportunity to operate like the wineries, have a tasting room, and sell directly to the public, which was not allowed.

Instead of quitting, he worked together with other small distillers and the New York State Farm Bureau to draft legislation and create a new license class in New York State. That was known as the New York State Farm Distilling Bill. There were just a handful of distillers at the time; people like Derek Grout from Harvest Spirits, Ralph Erenzo from Tuthilltown, Bill Martin from Montezuma Winery (Hidden Marsh Distillery) and Jason Grizzanti from Warwick Winery & Distillery (Black Dirt Distilling). They spent a lot of time in Albany lobbying for the bill. In the end, it was really the Farm Bureau, specifically Julie Suarez, who was chief lobbyist for the New York Farm Bureau, who got it to pass, because the Bureau had the resources to draft the legislation the right way.

One of the brightest points regarding the upstate New York economy is the wine and agri-tourism associated with the Finger Lakes. These were big reasons for Brian and Jennifer to get involved in the distillery, since there was such significant room for growth. The main reason they ended up with their particular property is because of its location within the Finger Lakes Wine Country. Finger Lakes Distilling's location has one of the highest concentrations of wineries and visitation in the area.

When Brian started the business, one of the first things he attended was a Distilling Conference in Louisville, Kentucky. At the conference, he was at a cocktail party and noticed a guy dressed in overalls. Brian decided to talk to him, because he looked like it would be a fun conversation. Brian's last name is McKenzie, and as it turned out, the other gentleman was a McKenzie also, from Southern Alabama. His name was Thomas McKenzie. The two men hit it off. Thomas came from a line of moon-shiners on both sides of his family, and had a farming background, as well as experience working in breweries and wineries. Not only did both men share the same last name, they also shared a passion for high quality spirits. At the time they had no connection beyond spending time together at the conference, until plans for the distillery company Thomas was working for fell through. Thomas contacted Brian and came on board from day one as their distiller. Although Brian knows a lot about production, the day to day production falls within Thomas's realm and Brian focuses more on the business side of things.

The first spirit that they distilled was vodka. They have four acres of grapes on the property. They harvested in 2008 and held the wine until they got their still installed in late 2008. That wine was the first thing that went through the still.

Once the bill was passed that allowed the farm distilleries, they committed to their goal, got the property, and began what ended up being a more than two-year process of getting product to market.

They started distilling their full product line as soon as they began production. Knowing how important the tasting room would be to the success of their business, they kicked things off with seven products: vodka, flavored vodka, gin, corn whiskey and three liqueurs. They wanted to have enough variety and have something for everyone's taste. Today, they have 15 products.

They sell over 50% of their product at the distillery. It is a great benefit being able to create that face to face relationship with the customer. Forty-thousand people visited them last year, something made possible by the Farm Distilling License. Most of their visitors are from New York State and neighboring states, but they also get visitors from other countries.

You can find Finger Lakes Distilling-products in seven states. They work with Winebow, New York is their core market. New York City and Brooklyn have been huge with regard to their growth. They work with a number of prominent cocktail bars, but their best customers are the locavore restaurants. The cuisine of many of these restaurants are typically locally driven and they are working on making their bar menu the same.

Finger Lakes Distilling does not rush product to market. Even though they are a young company, they age their whiskey for three to four years in large-scale barrels, and also utilize methods that are typically used on a large scale in Kentucky. These methods include using sour mash and a continuous still for their whiskeys. In a lot of ways they are like a mini bourbon distillery from Kentucky, in the Finger Lakes.

ALL THE TASTES OF NEW YORK

**Finger Lakes Distilling Company products can be purchased at the following locations:**

Flatiron Wines
929 Broadway, New York, NY 10010

Union Square Wine & Spirits
140 4th Avenue, New York, NY 10013

Astor Wines & Spirits
399 Lafayette Street, New York, NY 10003

**Finger Lakes Distilling Company products can be enjoyed at the following locations:**

ABC Kitchen
35 East 18th Street, New York, NY 10003

Blue Hill
75 Washington Place, New York, NY 10011

Gramercy Tavern
42 East 20th Street, New York, NY 10003

Finger Lakes Distilling Company is located at **4676 Route 414, Burdett, NY 14818**

## WHISKEY GARNET COCKTAIL

(Compliments of Finger Lakes Distilling)
2 ounces McKenzie Pure Pot Still Whiskey (or McKenzie Rye Whiskey)
1 ounce freshly squeezed blood orange juice
2 dashes simple syrup
1/4 ounce Stirrings Blood Orange Bitters
Orange twist

Combine all ingredients in a shaker with ice. Shake and strain into a chilled martini glass. Garnish with orange twist. Use Pot Still for a lighter, fruitier cocktail. Use Rye for a richer, spicier cocktail.

## ORANGE SMOKE RECIPE

(Compliments of Marina Lizarralde)
2 ounces Lapsang Souchong-Infused Seneca Drums Gin
1/2 ounce Aperol
2 dashes Whiskey Barrel-Aged Bitters
Orange peel

For Lapsang Souchong-infused gin: Put 1 tablespoon of Lapsang Souchong tea in a pint Mason jar. Fill jar with gin. Let the mixture soak for 6-12 hours, tasting periodically until it is satisfactorily smoky. Strain out the tea leaves, and store at room temperature. Use as desired.

Mix infused gin, Aperol, and bitters in a shaker with ice. Shake and strain into a chilled martini glass.

Bend and spritz the orange peel over the drink, then rub the rim of the glass with the peel to coat with orange oil. Drop orange peel in drink.

## WILD BERRY HARVEST

(Compliments of Finger Lakes Distilling)
2 ounces Vintner's Wild Berry Vodka
1/2 ounce Cointreau
4 ounces white grape juice
1/2 ounce simple syrup
1/4 ounce orange juice
Grapes

Combine all ingredients in a shaker with ice. Shake and strain into a chilled martini glass. Garnish with grapes.

# GLENROSE SPIRITS

James and Matthew Sloboda are a father-and-son team and co-owners of Glenrose Spirits. Their distillery is located in North Rose, New York. Small-batch producers of fruit brandy and malt whiskey, their products are distilled from apples which grow abundantly in Wayne County, where they are located.

James and Matthew both have very unique backgrounds that led them down the path to distilling. James is an electrical engineer who is also very mechanically inclined. Matthew went to culinary school and has been a professional chef for 14 yrs. He is also a private chef and head de cuisine of a very high-end estate.

Four years earlier, it occurred to James and Matthew that they should consider having a family business. Matthew was aware that things were changing with the creation of the Farm Distillery Act, and thought that the timing was perfect to open a distillery. Matthew's philosophy is that "when times are good, people drink; when times are bad, people drink more." It seemed like a very good business to be in.

They were both very hands-on in the creation of their business, in every step from building to distilling. For the distillery, they had the ground prepared and had a local Mennonite construction company come in to put up the frame of the building, then another to pour the concrete. After all of this, James and

**GLENROSE SPIRITS**

Matthew did the electrical, plumbing, panels, and other details.

Also having quite a bit of experience with brewing, Matthew has an incredible sense of taste and smell that has been of tremendous value to the business. The first spirit that they created was distilled from maple syrup, which provided a basis of understanding regarding what they wanted to create and the type of flavor profile that they wanted to achieve. With their very specific strengths, they make the perfect team.

With their commitment to use 100% New York State ingredients, all of their fruit is sourced locally. During the winter, when the fresh fruit season is over, they work with Empire Fruit Growers, whose facility is approximately five minutes away. When they discovered how many apple farms there are in Wayne County, James and

Matthew wanted to take advantage of what is so abundantly available, while supporting local farmers they have known for many years.

One of Glenrose Spirit's most popular products is their Apple Shine, which is also considered Apple Jack or Apple Brandy. Their Apple Shine is pot and column distilled in small batches, producing an extraordinarily smooth flavor with light aromas of apple.

They also use an apple base for their gin, as opposed to a grain base. Their Snow Devil Gin is a New World gin that is distilled with eight botanicals including elderflower, a botanical not typically used in gin. This gin derived its name from a mini twister that spiraled through the field where their distillery now sits. The memory of that image remained vivid in their minds and inspired the name Snow Devil. Their gin was a success after only two tries. It is created from distilling their Apple Shine to 90-proof and steeping the botanicals for numerous hours. In this way there are more botanical oils left to add their own distinct and unique flavors.

Their White Wolf is a column-distilled grain spirit made from a blend of four malted New York State grains.

The Pear Eau Du Vie Brandy is in its second year of production. This product is double-pot-distilled, with the pears fermented and distilled in the skins as they do with their apples. Their Pear Eau Du Vie is made with 100% pear.

Glenrose Spirits is completely self-financed, and they are working on increasing their volume. They are very much still in their research and development stage, and are working on solidifying their product line. They have also recently added absinthe to their product line. Hyssop, anise, fennel, small and large wormwood, and lemon balm all come together to give the absinthe its color and flavor.

In 2015, they will release their Dry House Apple Brandy, which is aged in used rye whiskey barrels. Their plan is to add an additional 2,000 square feet in the near future, to allow for increased capacity and barrels.

ALL THE TASTES OF NEW YORK

GLENROSE SPIRITS

Glenrose Spirits products can be purchased at the following locations:

**Irondequoit Liquor**
525 Titus Avenue, Rochester, NY 14617

**Lisa's Liquor Barn**
2157 Penfield Road, Penfield, NY 14526

**Andrew's Wine Cellar**
193 West 1st Street, Oswego, NY 13126

Glenrose Spirits products can be enjoyed at the following locations:

**Docker's Seafood & Grille**
6483 Catchpole Shore Road, North Rose, NY 14516

**Lento Restaurant**
274 Goodman Street, Rochester, NY 14607

**Pultneyville Grill**
4135 Mill Street, Williamson, NY 14538

You can visit the distillery for tastings and purchases on Sundays from 12 PM - 4 PM or by appointment. Glenrose Spirits is located at 5052 Covell Road, North Rose, NY 14516

# APPLE COUNTRY SPIRITS - TREE VODKA

**D**avid DeFisher is the founder of Apple Country Spirits (ACS), home of Tree Vodka. The distillery is located on a fourth-generation family fruit farm, DeFisher Fruit Farms, started by his great-grandfather in the early 1900s. Today, David still farms with his father, William.

They own 800 acres, a large portion of which is planted with fruit such as apples, cherries, pears, peaches, prunes, plums and, most recently, raspberries. They also grow pluots, which are a cross between a plum and an apricot. Their intention is to have different distilled spirits made from these fruits.

Five years ago, David and his wife, Christine, were thinking about what to do with all of the fruit they grow and the land that they own. They wanted to bring more of the direct consumer dollar to the farming operation, rather than wholesale all of the fruit they grow and not get the money it is worth. They ended up taking a distilling course at Cornell University that was all about farm distilling. It was exactly what they were looking for.

As they did the research, they began to realize that there were a very small number of people doing distillates from fruit-based raw products in this country. It is very common in Europe, but not in the United States.

Since they already had the raw product, it would become a value-added component to what they were already doing. As they began to look into equipment, they learned that most craft stills were made overseas. After a lot more research, they found

APPLE COUNTY SPIRITS

APPLE COUNTY SPIRITS
IN PHOTO: DAVID DEFISHER FOUNDER OF APPLE COUNTRY SPIRITS (LEFT)COLLIN MCCONVILLE HEAD DISTILLER (RIGHT)

a company named Vendome Copper and Brass in Louisville, Kentucky, a 104-year-old family-owned company which has been building distilling equipment for many years. This discovery was very important to the DeFishers, due to their commitment to buying as much American-made equipment for the operation as possible. Vendome worked with them closely to create a still for a company their size, since most of their clients were significantly larger. They also made their spirit safe, shaped like an apple, out of 100% copper; a personal touch that is very elegant and representative of their brand.

As ACS began to receive their equipment, they started to build and determine the appropriate specifications for their distillery. Although their tasting room was not part of the original business plan, as things progressed, they realized that their distillery could become a popular place for people to visit. They were right. They are now planning on adding a partyroom, since events have become a large part of their business.

In 2014, Apple Country Spirits' solar energy system was installed. They are now producing their own green energy, and the entire operation is powered by their solar array. Ninety-five percent of all of their equipment in the distilling/juicing process was made locally or in the USA.

Their head distiller, Collin McConville, has been distilling apple products for six years and has been a tremendous asset in the production of their product line. They have recently added hard cider production as well. Rootstock-Cider is the newest product to join their lineup. It is a semi-sweet hard cider made with a proprietary blend of apples grown by DeFisher Fruit Farms.

Tree Vodka is a 100%-apple-based vodka, not apple flavored. Therefore, it is also naturally gluten-free. It is neutral, yet slightly sweet on the end. There's about 50 pounds of apples in each bottle. There are currently two flavors of Tree Vodka: Peach Tree and Raspberry Tree. Peach Tree starts with their Tree Vodka with the extract created from their own peaches. Raspberry Tree starts with their Tree Vodka with extract created from their own raspberries.

They also have an un-aged Apple Jack, and their recently-released two-year Aged Apple Jack. Their Aged Apple Jack is aged in a 55-gallon oak barrel, like a whiskey or bourbon, and made with apples from their 100-proof un-aged apple jack. There will also be a five-year version of the aged applejack.

They offer a line of fruit brandies as well, referred to as an Eau Du Vie. They are made from 100% Bartlett pears, tart

ALL THE TASTES OF NEW YORK

cherries, and European plums.

Everything they make at ACS is fruit-based and naturally gluten-free. Fruit is a very expensive raw product, but with the abundance of fruit available to them, it was definitely the way to go!

ALL THE TASTES OF NEW YORK

## THE HONEYMOON

2 ounces Apple Country Sprits'
Applejack, 100-proof
1/2 ounce Benedictine
1/2 ounce Orange Curacao
1/2 ounce fresh lemon juice
Lemon peel for garnish

In a cocktail shaker, combine Applejack, Benedictine, Orange Curacao and lemon juice with ice. Shake. Serve in a rocks glass with lemon peel for garnish.

**Tree Vodka is located at 3274 Eddy Road, Williamson, NY 14589**

**Tree Vodka can be purchased at the following locations:**

Borisal Liquor & Wine
468 4th Avenue, Brooklyn, NY 11215

Landmark Wine & Sake
167 West 23rd Street, New York, NY 10011

Ryan's Wine & Liquor
234 William Floyd Parkway, Shirley, NY 11967

**Tree Vodka can be enjoyed at the following locations:**

The Smith
956 2nd Avenue, New York, NY 10022

Watkins Glen Harbor Hotel
16 North Franklin Street, Watkins Glen, NY 14891

Seneca Brew & Smokehouse
4516 West Lake Road, Geneva, NY 14456

## GREYHOUND

2 ounces Original Tree Vodka
4 ounces grapefruit juice
Splash of sparkling wine or hard cider

In a rocks glass, combine Tree Vodka, grapefruit juice and ice. Top off with sparkling wine or hard cider.

## RASPBERRY VODKA GIMLET

2 ounces Raspberry Tree Vodka
1/2 ounce lime juice
1 lime wedge

Combine Tree Vodka, lime juice and ice in a cocktail shaker. Serve in a chilled martini glass. Garnish with lime wedge.

# THE NOBLE EXPERIMENT - OWNEY'S RUM

**B**ridget Firtle comes from a long line of Brooklyn-based, small-business owners. She went to business school and started studying finance because she was naturally good with numbers. After she went to graduate school and got her MBA in finance, she went to work for a hedge fund on their consumer staples team. They were responsible for covering companies that were in food, beverage, alcohol, and tobacco. Because she enjoyed working at bars and restaurants throughout school, she was drawn towards investments in food and beverages.

After a win with a stock that owned a beer brand, the hedge fund manager fell in love with the alcohol category, and she worked her way into becoming the global alcoholic beverage analyst for the fund. She then spent approximately five years researching and investigating in global beer, wine, and spirits. It was a lot of bottoms-up

research, hanging out with sales guys and bartenders and really trying to get the pulse of trends. She did it all, including sitting down and interacting with senior management of multi-national alcohol companies. As she observed what was happening with the resurgence of the domestic distiller in the United States, she became enamored with the idea and became fascinated by the people behind it.

With the realization of where the trends were heading and the proliferation of the industry, due to the change

in legislation on a state-by-state basis, it was becoming clear that a movement was beginning. With the history of beer and spirits prior to Prohibition, Bridget had a vision to bring rum distilling back to the northeast, but specifically to New York.

Rum was America's first spirit, and Staten Island was home to the first rum distillery. With sugar cane molasses being brought up from the Caribbean by the British Navy and being distilled in New York, big business was being built around it. The molasses tax of 1764, which was imposed by the British, made the rum business unprofitable.

After the Revolution, distillers lost access to the molasses that was coming up from the British Navy, because the United States was now independent, and people began to grow grains as they moved west. They started to distill whiskey from their grains and it became known as America's first spirit, though it was, in fact, rum.

Being fascinated by this rich history and seeing all of the distillers making gins, whiskeys and vodkas, Bridget wanted to be part of the group to bring back rum distilling.

"Rum is a challenging category, but the challenge creates an opportunity to educate people on the history of rum and how it is made in different parts of the world in different ways. We could disrupt the rum category by doing something totally unique with unique ingredients and a propriety technique," Bridget told me.

In 2011, while assessing the next step in her career in finance, Bridget realized that what really excited her was looking into the funding of small businesses and startups. She began to gather very valuable information while interviewing and networking. The turning point for Bridget came one day in June 2011, when she was watching a TED talk by a professor at Stanford University. He was speaking to the MBA students about venture capital. His topic addressed the flawed thinking of simply wanting to be a venture capitalist when you have never run a business. "You need to run a business to know how to evaluate someone else's business plan," he said. His words struck a chord in Bridget. The idea of not being afraid to fail and taking risk resonated with Bridget. She realized that if there was ever a time in her life to take a risk it would be now, and so she started writing a business plan that day. She then spent the next six months hashing out her plan, figuring out how to fund it, and holding on to her paychecks for as long as she could. She left the fund at the end of 2011.

The Farm Distillery License allows for direct sale; however, to qualify, you have to use ingredients that are 75% New York State-grown. Since sugar cane is not grown in New York, her business in particular does not benefit from that particular advantage. However, the new law that Governor Cuomo recently signed (November 13th, 2014), allows cocktails to be served in the distilleries' tasting rooms. One of her goals is to start making a farm product in-house that will only be sold at her establishment.

Owney's Rum is the first liquor of The Noble Experiment, named after Owney Madden, a Prohibition-era mobster, bootlegger, and notorious rum-runner. In keeping with every aspect of the business being rooted in the history of New York. Bridget knew that she wanted a high-ester-content rum with a lot of flavor. These are molasses-based rums that are generally native to Jamaica. However, her rum is also influenced by agricole-style rums of the French Caribbean. To qualify as rum, the spirit must be made from sugar cane. Owney's Rum is made from a first boil molasses, which is a by-product of sugar refining.

Owney's Rum does not include any added sugar or coloring, artificial flavor, or preservatives. It is not barrel-aged. Their philosophy is to use the best quality ingredients they can source, and curate those ingredientsin the best way possible, using a unique technique. This enables them to create a spirit that has a lot of character, body, and depth.

After trying a number of different molasses and yeast strains, Bridget settled on only three ingredients: filtered New York City water, Grade-A, non-GMO sugar cane molasses from Florida and Louisiana, and proprietary

yeast. Bridget spent a considerable amount of time getting familiar with what she wanted to create. This meant her trial period was not very long, since she was well-versed in how to achieve her desired style of rum. It just became a question of fine tuning.

Her philosophy revolves around the power of fermentation. The Noble Experiment does a five-day cold fermentation, which Bridget believes preserves and develops flavor at that stage through esterification. This is a chemical process where alcohols and acids bind to form aldehydes and where you get a lot of fruity aromas, banana notes, and even some smoke. They then distill what was fermented in a pot-column hybrid still at a low rectification (about 164-proof) in order to showcase the flavors created during the fermentation. This distillation level is very unique for a white rum, and similar to tequila, whiskey, or agricole rums.

Owney's can be found at numerous NYC bars, liquor stores and restaurants; in Union Square, Flatiron, the Meatpacking District, the Lower East Side, and Brooklyn. Specific locations are listed at the end of this chapter.

NICK JOHNSON

**The Noble Experiment is located at 23 Meadow Street, Brooklyn, NY 11206**

## MAI TAI

2 ounces Owney's
1/2 ounce Curacao
1/4 ounce orgeat
1/4 ounce simple syrup
2 dashes of vanilla extract

**Fill cocktail shaker with ice. Add Owney's, Curacao, orgeat, simple syrup. Shake. Serve in a rocks glass.**

## THE SMASH

2 ounces Owney's
2-3 sprigs of mint
1 slice of lemon
1 bar spoon of sugar
Soda

**Muddle sugar, lemon and mint at bottom of rocks glass, add Owney's then ice and club soda floater.**

## CLASSIC DAIQUIRI

2 ounces Owney's
1 ounce fresh lime juice
3/4 ounce simple syrup
1 lime wheel

**Shake vigorously and double strain into coupe glass. Garnish with lime wheel.**

**Owney's Rum can be purchased at the following locations:**

Astor Wine & Spirits
399 Lafayette Street, (at East 4th St.), New York, NY 10003

Atlantic Cellars
988 Atlantic Avenue, Brooklyn, NY 11238

Brooklyn Wine Exchange
138 Court Street, Brooklyn, NY 11201

**Owney's Rum can be enjoyed at the following locations:**

ABC Kitchen
35 East 18th Street, New York, NY 10003

The Tippler
425 West 15th Street, New York, NY 10011

The Standard Hotel
848 Washington at 13th Street, New York, NY 10014

# DOC'S ALL NATURAL SPIRITS

Doc's All Natural Spirits was originally founded in the Herson's Brownstone basement in Harlem, by Kevin Herson and his wife Stacey. As they researched how to start a distillery, they realized that this could be a good and viable business, and they certainly had a great ground floor space that lent itself perfectly to testing their vision.

When Kevin and Stacey were trying to determine what they wanted to distill, they tested a number of spirits, such as moonshine and whiskey, and they experimented to determine what would best represent them.

Growing up in South Africa, Kevin's love of culture led him to travel the world and embrace each culture's customs through the food and drinks that best represented them. After a number of trials, it occurred to them that absinthe was the way to go. They were both absinthe drinkers, and no one else was distilling absinthe in New York City at the time.

Realizing that the expectation of absinthe is to have a very heavy anise profile, they knew that they wanted to make their brand more approachable and palatable by cutting back on the anise. It was important to reach as wide an audience as possible.

Doc's Absinthe is made with New York grain, sugar, water, and yeast. The fermented liquid is then put into the still with herbs. After the process of distillation, additional herbs are added with fresh mint, which imparts the green coloring typically associated with green absinthe. Each batch is bottled individually, waxed, sealed and hand-labeled by Kevin.

After going through the licensing process, they decided to move their business to their current location, which is in the Bedford-Stuyvesant section of Brooklyn. The move also allowed them to increase production. They are currently in the process of upscaling their operation to allow them to commit full time to this endeavor.

The response that they have been receiving from their product has been tremendous. Their story is very appealing and resonates with the people who are aware of what they were doing. There is tremendous pride in having an all-American company that is local, and makes everything from scratch. Their customers take pride in that.

With regard to their flavor profile, Kevin's background in cooking was very helpful. His recipes were all trial and error as he tested batch after batch. Eventually he pieced together the desirable components of each recipe that appealed to him, until he came up with one that best represented the brand.

They are in 19 liquor stores to date. Most are in Brooklyn, though there are a few in Manhattan and upstate New York.

DOC'S ALL NATURAL SPIRITS

DOC'S ALL NATURAL SPIRITS
IN PHOTO: KEVIN HERSON

**Doc's All Natural Spirits can be purchased from the following locations:**

Sussex Wine & Spirits
300 East 42nd Street, New York, NY 10016

Whiskey & Wine off 69
1321 2nd Avenue, New York, NY 10021

St. Mark's Wine & Liquor
16 St. Mark's Place, New York, NY 10003

**Doc's All Natural Spirits can be enjoyed at the following locations:**

Eleven Madison Park
11 Madison Park, New York, NY 10010

Blue Smoke
116 East 27th Street, New York, NY 10016

Harlem Public
3612 Broadway, New York, NY 10031

## DOC'S SPARKLING LEMONADE

1 ounce Doc's Absinthe
Splash of soda
Squeeze of lemon
Ice

**Add ingredients and serve in rocks glass.**

## CHINA BREW

1 1/2 ounces hot gingertea
1 ounce Doc's Absinthe
Squeeze of lemon
1 teaspoon of honey

**Steep ginger tea, then add Doc's Absinthe, lemon, honey and stir.**

## ST. MARK'S SAZERAC

1/2 ounce of Doc's Green Absinthe
1 1/2 ounces of bourbon
1 sugar cube
1 teaspoon of fresh squeezed orange juice
2 dashes of rhubarb bitters
Twist of orange peel

**Shake ingredients and serve in a highball glass.**

# HIDDEN MARSH DISTILLERY

The story of Hidden Marsh Distillery begins with George and Virginia Martin and their two sons, Ed and Bill. In 1994, all management personnel at the steam station where George was employed were forced into retirement. George decided to become a full-time beekeeper, which quickly converted from a hobby into a full-time business.

By the time Bill, George's second son, finished college, George and Ed, his first son, had a relatively well-established honey business. Their honey production and pollination business grew to contain 2,000 hives which made 90 to 100 tons of honey a year. Finding a different way to use their honey, Bill began making mead (honey wine) while spending a lot of time taking their honey to Greenmarkets in New York City and Brooklyn.

In 1999, the family took the leap and applied for a farm winery license. With this, their commercial production of honey wine began. The Martin Honey Farm and Meadery continued to grow, and when Bill's father was made aware of a method to make mead which allowed it to go much faster to market, it increased the volume of business.

Living in what is referred to as the fruit belt of New York State, it seemed like a natural progression for the Martins to begin making wine from various fruits. With the addition of grape wines, their dynamic portfolio continued to grow. Montezuma Winery was created when they purchased their current property in February 2001. What was originally a storefront to sell their products is now the hub of production for their wineries and distilleries.

Bill is a natural when it comes to the craft of wine and spirits. His excitement about experimenting and trying new things has been a proven success. At Montezuma Winery you will find 51 different wines, at Hidden Marsh Distillery you will find over nine spirit varieties, and at their newest winery, Idol Ridge, you will find 23 different wines. This list will continue to grow since new products are already in production.

In 2007, Montezuma Winery started thinking about making fruit brandy and Eau de Vie. At the same time, they were lobbying in Albany for the laws to change. Changing these laws would make it easier for them to distill. There were six distilleries in the state at the time. Even sourcing their still was challenging, since it was hard to find a manufacturer that would make a still appropriate for the volumes of a small distiller. In addition, none of them had any training, so the learning curve was something to be considered.

With the laws in the process of changing, the Martins purchased a still with a column, allowing them to make vodka. Their 400-liter Christian Carl column pot still has two columns, consisting of a four-plate column for high-end brandy and whiskey production, and a 21-plate column for premium vodka production. Being the first of its kind in the Finger Lakes

CHRISTINE ALEXANDER
IN PHOTO: BILL MARTIN

region, Hidden Marsh Distillery was one of the pioneers in the field of artisan distilling in New York State. Each batch is a hands-on process and takes on a more artistic form to produce high-quality premium spirits.

Their first spirit was Apple Brandy, made during the experimentation process. They actually still have an apple brandy, aging from 2008.

Since they did not have mash tuns at that time, as they were determining what to make vodka out of, it occurred to them to distill honey. This was the birth of Bee Vodka. In 2011, they began working on the making of beer for whiskey.

Now, Hidden Marsh Distillery's repertoire consists of bourbon, rye whiskey, gin, apple vodka, and jalapeno-infused vodka. Their corn whiskey, Judd's Wreckin' Ball, has been awarded the #1 Spirit in the State for 2014. This is all topped with spectacular liqueurs that express the local flavor.

With regard to how they developed their flavor profile, they take all direction from their products. They do not try to make it into anything other than what it wants to be. For the most

CHRISTINE ALEXANDER

part they are happy with their first mead and honey vodka. The same philosophy exists with their brandy. Bill creates a product with an end-goal in mind, but also allows that product to steer him in the direction it would like to go.

"Our goal is to make the best quality spirits that we can produce. We have the world's best still and top-notch base ingredients. We just help to hold the sails and steer the ship," Bill said.

Because Montezuma Winery has existed for over 14 years, there is a bit of blending of the brands between Montezuma Winery and Hidden Marsh Distillery. They are working on rebranding Hidden Marsh Distillery, since initially it was an add-on to the business. As a brand which is rapidly growing, restructuring is in the works. The vast variety of Hidden Marsh Distillery's spirits is sold through their tasting room and other local venues.

Hidden Marsh Distillery is located at 2981 U.S. Route 20, in Seneca Falls, within the Montezuma Winery facility

HIDDEN MARSH DISTILLERY
IN PHOTO: BILL MARTIN CO-OWNER HIDDEN MARSH DISTILLERY

MONTEZUMA WINERY

## SKEETER JUICE

2 ounces Judd's Wreckin' Ball Corn Whiskey
12 ounces lemonade

**Mix ingredients together in a mason jar.**

## HOT BERRY BREEZE

4 parts Bee Hot Pepper-Flavored Vodka
1 part raspberry liqueur
1 part cranberry juice
2 raspberries

**Fill a highball glass to the rim with ice cubes. Pour all the ingredients over the ice. Garnish with raspberries.**

Hidden Marsh Distillery Spirits can be purchased at the following locations:

Harbor View Wine & Liquor
936 North Clinton Street, Syracuse, NY 13204

Liquor & Wine Warehouse
25 Smithfield Boulevard, Plattsburgh, NY 12901

Headley's Liquor Barn
820 Routes 5 & 20, Geneva, NY 14456

## CITRUS SMASH

2 ounces Bee Vodka
1 ounce Grand Marnier
1/2 lemon, quartered
3-4 mint leaves
1/2 ounce honey syrup (4 parts honey to 1 part water)

**Muddle lemon, mint, and honey syrup. Add vodka, Grand Marnier, and ice. Shake well and double strain into a chilled cocktail glass.**

# ALBANY DISTILLING COMPANY

**M**att Jager and John Curtin were friends well before they went into business together. Initially, they wanted to open a bar, and briefly considered having a brew pub. Since there was already a great brew pub in town, and considering the challenges of funding their own brew pub (since, by nature, the bar/restaurant category is risky), they began to reassess the idea. They also wanted to create a business that they were passionate about.

On the other hand, both Matt and John were fans of whiskey. It occurred to them to revise the plan by taking out the bar and restaurant component, focusing on distilling. It was still not easy to raise the necessary capital, but they were now embarking upon a venture that they were passionate about. That made all the difference.

Albany Distilling Company was founded in 2011, and is located in

downtown Albany, not far from the site of the city's original 18th-century distillery. The team at Albany Distilling Company is as unique as the products that they create. Matt Jager is a college professor for information systems and marketing at the college of St. Rose. John Curtin is a retired high school English teacher. John's wife, Brooke Curtin, manages their marketing and sales. Rick Sicari is their distiller, who has a background in business, and began his career as a brewer. Before Rick was brought on board at the Albany Distilling Company, he was looking at the market of craft beer versus the market of craft distillers and he noticed the tremendous increase in distilleries. He decided he wanted to be part of the development of the craft distillers' movement.

Being a distiller is, by no means, an easy way to make a living. Matt and John consider themselves fortunate to live in New York, where the state government allows the process of distilling to be

ALL THE TASTES OF NEW YORK
IN PHOTO: JOHN CURTIN - CO-OWNER ALBANY DISTILLING COMPANY

easier, so people like them can get the support they need. With the influx of craft distillers over the last few years, their feeling is that the more craft distillers there are, the better for their company, because New York State as a whole is being placed on the map.

Since neither Matt nor John came from a family of distillers, they learned their craft through trial and error, visiting distilleries and attending workshops. They went to Chicago, and visited Koval when they were making a decision on what kind of still to purchase, which also allowed them the opportunity to obtain some hands-on experience.

When they started distilling, their first product was their Coal Yard New Make Whiskey, followed by their Ironweed

Bourbon. Although they are both big fans of rye whiskey, they acknowledge that bourbon had more name recognition, so they came up with a formulation of 60% corn and 25% rye. This allowed them to create a more familiar product, yet one that was more representative of them. Their Ironweed Bourbon Whiskey captures both the essence of a bygone era and the spirit of modern innovation.

Their Coal Yard New Make Whiskey is an expression of the true nature of craft distilling. Once collected, it is kept briefly in a used cooperage in order to best preserve the smooth, fresh flavor of the grain.

They also have a rum product called Quackenbush Still House Rum. They are unable to sell and taste their rum at the distillery, since the New York State Farm Distillery License does not allow them to do tastings of any product not made primarily from New York State ingredients. However, their A1 license allows them to produce it. Quackenbush Still House Rum an Original Albany Rum pays homage to Albany's first distillery, which was established in the mid-18th century and stood a short distance from where Albany Distilling Company stands today. In the late 1700s, the Quackenbush family made an un-aged rum from Caribbean molasses and Hudson River water, fermented with wild yeasts in open wooden vessels. Although they use modern equipment, better yeast, and a more suitable water supply, Albany Distilling follows the same recipe and methods of their predecessors.

When asked if they would venture into other products, Matt and John said that, at this time, they are focusing on their bourbon and rye whiskey, which are their rock-star products. Their rye got them a gold medal at ACDA in 2013 and they are focused on perfecting it.

Half of their sales are made at the distillery, and most of their territory is in the Albany area. To this point, they have been able to sell all of their products by self-distributing, thereby remaining relatively local. They do use a distributor for their rum.

Currently, they are working with a coffee-roasting company called Death Wish, whose claim is that they make the world's strongest coffee, a dark roast coffee. Death Wish uses Albany Distilling Company's used whiskey and rum barrels, putting the unroasted green beans into the barrels. The beans absorb all of the liquid after a few weeks. The flavor that the beans absorb makes amazing coffee.

They are also working with a local beer company that is next door, called C.H. Evans. C.H. Evans is aging their beer in Albany Distilling Company's used barrels. I was fortunate enough during my visit to witness them blending the barrels to determine what their flavor profile will be for their upcoming release.

Look out for their collaborations and enjoy all of the elements that make Albany Distilling Company unique!

**Albany Distilling Company is located at 78 Montgomery Street, Albany, NY 12207**

ALL THE TASTES OF NEW YORK

## MOSS COAL MULE

2 ounces Coal Yard Bourbon
3/4 ounce Adirondack ginger ale
1 lime
1/2 ounce fresh ginger

**Combine in a highball glass.**

## IRONWEED OLD FASHIONED

2 ounces Ironweed Rye
2 Luxardo maraschino cherries, muddled
1 orange slice
2 dashes orange bitters
1 ounce soda

**Combine ingredients in highball glass.**

Albany Distilling Company products can be purchased at the following locations:

Capital Wine& Spirits
348 State Street, Albany, NY 12210

All Star Wine & Spirits
579 Troy Schenectady Road, Latham, NY 12110

Crush & Cask Wine & Spirits
170 South Broadway, Saratoga Springs, NY 12866

Albany Distilling Company products can be enjoyed at the following locations:

677 Prime
677 Broadway, Albany, NY 12207

Stockade Tavern
313 Fair Street, Kingston, NY 12401

The Gaf
1804 2nd Avenue, New York, NY 10128

## KENNEDY SOUR

(Compliments of Robert Mack at The Speakeasy in Albany, NY)
1 1/2 ounces Ironweed Bourbon
3/4 ouncefresh ruby red grapefruit juice
2 dashes of lemon bitters
2 dashes of grapefruit bitters
1/2 ounce ginger beer
1 lemon twist
1 candied wrapped ginger cube

**Combine over ice in high-ball glass. Top with ginger beer. Garnish with lemon twist-wrapped candied ginger cube.**

# HARVEST SPIRITS

**T**he vision for Harvest Spirits was created with the realization that vodka can be made from apples. This created a value-added product. Derek Grout and his then partner, Tom Crowell, attended a seminar held by Christian Carl in New Hampshire. Tom, who is the current owner of Chatham Brewing, suggested going on a weekend of distilling to learn more about the business.

At the seminar, Derek and Tom met the team from Tuthilltown Spirits, who had just received their license. Tuthilltown Spirits was seeking an apple farmer to provide them with apples for cider. Derek and Tom did a handshake deal with Tuthilltown Spirits, agreeing to provide the surplus apples from Derek's father's farm for cider and, in return, Tuthilltown would provide half the alcohol. This, of course, was easier said than done, since they could not transfer alcohol to Derek and Tom until they had a liquor license.

At that point, Derek and Tom realized they needed to pursue their own venture, because this was likely not a viable business relationship. With the realization that they needed to get a license to distill vodka and focus more on getting people to the farm, Harvest Spirits Farm applied for their farm license and began making its own products. In May 2008, the farm distillery opened for business.

Launched at the cliff of the financial crisis, it was the worst time to launch a new luxury product. With so many people facing unemployment, they were challenging times for Harvest Spirits. The business is very capital-intense and, with revenue not coming in at the same rate that it was going out, hard decisions needed to be made. After depleting his personal savings and facing challenges repaying debt, Derek bought out Tom, making Derek and his wife, Ashley, sole owners of Harvest Spirits.

Harvest Spirits has the distinction of being the first New York State farm distillery with a Class D license, making them one of the few distillers that grows their own raw materials. They began as farmers, and the distillery sits right on the farm itself.

Their Core Vodka was the first spirit they distilled. From that single product, they were able to create a range of

# HARVEST SPIRITS
## FARM DISTILLERY

products, all from fruit grown on their farm. They also make an Applejack, as well as cherry-and peach-infused versions and a number of other brandies.

The range of products that can be made at Harvest Spirits is endless, since they are so vertically integrated, from growing the fruit to distribution. Often what prompted what they were going to create and distill was a result of a surplus of fruit that was available. Most of their innovation is a result of opportunities that present themselves, not necessarily based upon seeking a new direction. This approach has served them well over the years.

Their latest venture is a single-malt whiskey. Two years before, there was a freeze, and there were no apples from Michigan to Maine. They were lucky to find apples that they could purchase,

but when they ran out, there was nothing to distill.

That January, they partnered with a brewer to make a beer that could be distilled into a whiskey. Fortunately they partnered with a very capable brewer, and it created a fantastic whiskey, due to come out in limited release in February 2015. It will be named John Henry Single-Malt Whiskey, after an employee from Jamaica, who has been working on their farm for four decades. Although their whiskey was in response to the challenge of not having any apples, their goal is to make their whiskey only in the winter with the same brewer, and age it for at least three years.

Their Cornelius Apple Jack was also named after the gentleman who presses their apple cider, who has also been with them for four decades. They think that it is a great way to honor the people

HARVEST SPIRITS
IN PHOTO: HARVEST SPIRITS CO-OWNERS ASHLEY HARTKA AND DEREK GROUT

Harvest Spirits is located at 3074 U.S. 9, Valatie, NY 12184

who work for them and have been contributing to the business for many years.

Derek believes that there are three types of people who get into this business. The first doesn't have a lot of money but has a lot of passion, the second has a lot of money and a lot of passion, and the third is someone who wants to preserve farming as a way of life and preserve open space.

Derek's family has been apple farmers for three generations and he would like it to extend beyond the fourth generation. He believes that businesses are transitioned from one generation to the next by creating a legacy product like brandy or other quality products, and passing down a trade and way of making money to the next generation.

## THE WISE SAGE

(Compliments of the Temple Bar in
New York, NY)
4 ounces of Core Vodka
6 fresh sage leaves
4 slices of fresh apple
2 ounces fresh squeezed lemon juice
3 teaspoons of fine sugar

**Muddle sage leaves. Shake
with ice. Strain into a
chilled martini glass. Garnish with apple slice.**

## JOHNNY APPLEJACK

(Compliments of Ashley & Derek of
Harvest Spirits)
2 shots Cornelius Applejack
1/2 shot fresh lemon
3 shots fresh apple cider
2 dashes of Angostura Bitters
1 ounce soda
1 lemon slice

**Stir and pour into an ice-
filled OldFashioned, top
with soda water. Garnish
with lemon slice.**

## THE BRAMBLY HEDGE

(Compliments of Robert Mack at
The Speakeasy in Albany, NY)
1 ounce Cornelius Applejack
1/2 ounce Nardini Amaro
1/2 ounce Vedrenne Super Cassis
1/2 ounce fresh lemon juice
4 ounces Fentiman's Ginger Beer

**Combine ingredients in a
shaker with ice and serve
in a highball glass.**

**Harvest Spirits products can
be purchased at the following
locations:**

Astor Wine & Spirits
399 Lafayette Street (at East 4th St.),
New York, NY 10003

Sherry Lehmann Wine & Spirits
505 Park Avenue, New York, NY
10022

67 Wine
179 Columbus Avenue, New York, NY
10023

**Harvest Spirits products can
be enjoyed at the following
locations:**

The Oyster Bar
Grand Central Terminal, 89 East 42nd
Street, New York, NY 10017

The Standard Hotel
848 Washington at 13th Street, New
York, NY 10014

The Plaza Hotel
768 5th Avenue, New York, NY 10019

# STILLTHEONE DISTILLERY

After college, Ed Tiedge went into the Marine Corp, where he remained for seven years as an artillery officer. He then went to business school and spent almost 20 years on Wall Street in fixed-income portfolios and bond trading. In 2008, the second hedge fund that Ed joined started to have liquidity problems, at which point he decided that there was something else he needed to do.

He knew that with his range of skills there were numerous ventures that he could explore. He knew he wanted to create a real product and, having a math and physics background, he initially thought it would be something that required engineering, mechanical or chemical processing. His first idea was to do something in biodiesel, but his passion for unique spirits fueled his curiosity and he stumbled upon the world of distilling.

In late 2008, he decided to search the term 'distillation', and a story came up in The New York Times about Tuthilltown Spirits, which had opened a few years earlier. That article prompted a more thorough search into the world of craft distilleries. The idea of opening a distillery was, in Ed's opinion at the time, kin to starting your own car company, as it did not seem like a small-business idea. "You think of all of the big companies that have tremendous capital, not as something that one or two people can do," Ed told me. However, as he started to come across the number of small distillers who were doing it, it completely changed his perspective.

Ed and his wife Laura live in Westchester, and they knew that they wanted their distillery to be in Westchester also. StillTheOne Distillery was a name inspired by Laura, who is also his Chief Tasting Officer and an avid gin drinker.

Ed began his journey into crafting

STILLTHEONE
DISTILLERY & SPIRITS
*Distilled From Honey*

COMB
VODKA

Comb Vodka

Comb 9 Gin

Comb Blossom

Comb White

Comb Jarhead Gin

Byram River Rum

spirits by studying distillation and vinification in California and working at a small winery and distillery in Cognac, France. He then began researching the production of mead, a honey wine that has been made since ancient times.

From his experience distilling wine into brandy, Ed began to formulate the process to distill honey wine into spirits. As they were working on determining what they wanted their product to taste like, the honey provided them with the direction that they needed to be unique. It took about six months with different varietals and combinations before they settled on what best represented them. Although honey is expensive, hard to work with, and difficult to ferment, the spirit that it produced was its own reward, in complexity and flavor. Their honey is made by bees that gather nectar from orange blossoms, and the unique character creates a perfectly balanced spirit. After finding the right varietal honey and yeast combinations and the precise distillation technique, they created their Comb Vodka.

Their next spirit was their gin. Since Laura is an avid gin drinker, if Ed was going to be a distiller, he had to distill gin. Their gin was a more interim process, once they settled on using a honey-distilled spirit. Laura was designated the chief tasting officer for the gin, and the reason that they call it Comb 9 is because, on the ninth version, Laura declared that she would now start drinking his gin!

Through not strictly a London Dry style, their Comb 9 Gin also does not conform to any particular style. They start with the essence of the honey spirit used in their Comb Vodka, and gently redistill it in small batches with juniper berries, lavender, fresh citrus, galangal, and other selected botanicals. It is very floral and deep, with an herbal and citrus finish.

Their Jarhead Gin, which is distilled with a blend of organic New York State wheat and honey, was inspired by a call Ed received in February 2011 from the Wounded Warrior Project, asking if he could donate a few bottles of spirits for an auction at an upcoming benefit. Ed immediately agreed, but wanted to do better than just drop off a few bottles. Ed formulated a new gin made in a single batch of 12 bottles, with handmade labels and a custom wood case, in acknowledgement of his service in the United States Marines. He called it Jarhead Gin. Their Jarhead Gin is bright and lively with juniper, coriander, fresh citrus, ginger, and botanicals.

Their 287 Whiskey was made in partnership with a local brewery, Captain Lawrence Beer, when the realization struck them that both beer and whiskey are made from grain. Then why not make whiskey from beer made by the neighboring brewery? The only thing he knew for certain about his whiskey was that he wanted to work with a brewer. When they approached Captain Lawrence's owner, Scott Vacarro, with the idea, he sent them thousands of gallons of his Westchester Pale Ale

to distill into whiskey. With that, 287 Single Malt Whiskey was born. Named after the highway that connects Still-TheOne Distillery and the Captain Lawrence Brewery, 287 Single Malt Whiskey is carefully distilled to capture the nuance of the malted barley, and then matured in new oak barrels.

Their Westchester Wheat Whiskey is made from 100% New York State wheat. No corn. They wanted to let the grain express itself in the whiskey. Their philosophy is to let the character of what they are making express itself completely in the product.

Ed generally prefers to age his whiskey in larger barrels, since he is concerned that in smaller barrels there is too much extraction, and the more subtle characteristics do not come through. Subtle flavors like vanilla rarely ever come through in small barrel aging, and the chemical changes that occur over time as a whiskey ages make a significant difference in the final product.

The heart of their distillery is in the fermentation and distillation equipment, and the pride associated with being the first distillery in Westchester County. Ed is also part owner of Taconic Distillery, in Stantonville, NY.

**StillTheOne products can be purchased at the following locations:**

**First Avenue Vintner**
984 1st Avenue, New York, NY 10022

**Park Ave Liquor**
292 Madison Avenue, New York, NY 10017

**Gotham Wines & Spirits**
2517 Broadway, New York, NY 10025

**StillTheOne products can be enjoyed at the following locations:**

**Mark Hotel**
21 East 77thStreet, New York, NY 10021

**ABC Kitchen**
35 East 18th Street, New York, NY 10003

**Fort Defiance**
365 Van Brunt Street, Brooklyn, NY 11231

## KING BEE

1 teaspoon Darjeeling tea leaves
3 ounces Comb Vodka
1 1/2 ounces fresh lemon juice
2 ounces honey syrup*
1 thin slice of lemon

Sprinkle tea leaves over the vodka in a glass container, and set aside to steep for 30 minutes (for a party, use eight teaspoons tea for 750ml Comb Vodka). Strain the infused Comb Vodka. Add the strained vodka, lemon juice and honey syrup to a cocktail shaker. Add ice, cover and shake for 15 seconds. Strain into a cocktail glass and garnish with lemon slice.

*To make honey syrup: Mix 1 cup honey and 1 cup warm water.

**StillTheOne Distillery is located at 1 Martin Place, Port Chester, NY 10573**

## BEE STING SHOOTERS

2 ounces Comb Vodka
3/4 ounce Cointreau
1/2 ounce lime juice
1/4 ounce raspberry liqueur
1/4 ounce sour mix (3 parts sugar / 2 parts water / 1 part lemon juice)

Shake with ice and strain into shot glasses or pour over shaved ice in a cocktail glass.

## BEACH COMBER

1 1/2 ounces Comb Vodka
1/4 ounce triple sec
2 dashes maraschino liqueur
3/4 ounce lime juice

Add all ingredients to a shaker and shake about 10 times. Pour into a chilled glass. Surf's up!

# ORANGE COUNTY DISTILLERY

Orange County Distillery was founded by John Glebocki and Bryan Ensall. John is the owner of J. Glebocki Farms, a 120-acre fifth-generation farm in Goshen, New York, and Bryan is the owner of a lawn-care franchise that services all of Orange County, New York. During Christmas of 2012 both men realized that they had the same four months off, and acknowledged the opportunity that time was providing. With that, the first seeds of Orange County Distillery were planted.

Of the 120 acres of black dirt owned by J. Glebocki Farms, 20 acres are used

to grow the grains and sugar beets for their spirits and the botanicals for their gin. They also grow their own malt, barley, rye, and corn.

ORANGE COUNTY DISTILLERY

As a result, they are able to host tastings of their spirits at Greenmarket. Greenmarket operates farmers markets in NYC. Over 200 local farmers, fishers, and bakers sell what they grow, raise, catch, and bake themselves. Greenmarket is a program of GrowNYC, a privately-funded nonprofit organization. With their products coming 100% from their farm, Orange County Distillery is the only distillery that qualifies to do spirit tastings throughout NYC.

John and Bryan converted a 100-year-old barn to house their distillery and tasting room by building out everything themselves. The distillery is value added to the farm so, as the business grows, they will eventually move their tasting room and distillery into the larger building on the farm that currently stores their vegetables and grains.

Orange County Distillery vodka is distilled from sugar beets. This was one of the first products created by their team, and was an idea that John had due to having 6,000 pounds of sugar beets. Since the sugar beets grow well for them, they thought that it was a great option and it also has a very unique flavor profile, adding distinctness to their product. It is the ideal sipping vodka and was first brought to market in October 2014.

Their corn whiskey, which also went to market in October 2014, is made from 88% corn and 12% barley. It is an un-aged whiskey that perfectly captures the sweetness of the corn.

Their first batch of bourbon was made in May 2014 from 88% corn and 12% barley. Aged for five months, their bourbon has hints of caramel, orange zest, cinnamon, and oak.

Their Orange County Distillery Gin is made from corn and botanicals, all grown on the farm. Their gin has flavors of juniper, citrus mint, coriander, lemon

balm, angelica root, staghorn sumac and lavender.

Starting as small as they did, it gave John and Bryan the opportunity to test and try as many different versions of their products as they desired, until they settled on what they felt best represented them.

They are being contacted by numerous restaurants and liquor stores in the county, and are working on keeping supply and demand in sync, which presents certain challenges being that they pride themselves on growing everything they make. The only things they purchase are their bottles, barrels, and labels.

ORANGE COUNTY DISTILLERY

**Orange County Distillery**
**Products can be purchased from**
**the following locations:**

Goshen Plaza Liquor
92 Clowes Avenue, Goshen, NY
10924

Grape Connection
4958 Route 17M, New Hampton, NY
10958

High Withers Wine & Spirits
83 West Main Street, Goshen, NY
10924

---

**Orange County Distillery**
**Products can be enjoyed at the**
**following locations:**

Blue Hill New York
75 Washington Place, New York, NY
10011

Blue Hill at Stone Barns
630 Bedford Road, Pocantico Hills, NY
10591

Glenmere Mansion
634 Pine Hill Road, Chester, NY 10918

# BLACK DIRT DISTILLERY

lack Dirt Distillery was founded by Jason Grizzanti and Jeremy Kidde in March 2012. However, Jason and Jeremy have both been making and selling distilled spirits since 2002, at the Warwick Valley Winery and Distillery, which was started by Jason's father, Joseph, in 1994. Warwick Winery and Distillery was the first winery to obtain a New York State fruit distillery license.

Before they shifted their focus from wine to spirits, they were producing approximately 75,000 cases of hard cider. At the time, their cider was being sold in 20 states, and each of their distributors was requesting their soon-to-be-released bourbon. The problem was that the amount of bourbon they had was very small relative to the demand.

In order to meet the demand for their Black Dirt Bourbon and Black Dirt Apple Jack, a product of the Warwick Valley Winery and Distillery,

they constructed a 4,000-square-foot distillery in Pine Island, New York in 2013. This new distillery has the capability to produce 30-40 times the amount of product that was distilled at Warwick Valley Winery and Distillery. Black Dirt takes its name from the dark, fertile soil left by an ancient glacial lake that once covered thousands of acres of upstate New York. Perfectly suited for growing crops such as corn. This black dirt has never been used for bourbon production until now.

At Black Dirt Distillery, there are three silos that hold corn, malted barley, and rye. Most of their products are made with variations of these ingredients. The red heirloom corn, called Bloody Butcher, will be used to make a unique whiskey that has not yet been released. This whiskey is in the middle of production. As a general rule, they typically do not release any of their products for at least two years.

Being that Black Dirt Distillery was the first distiller of spirits in New York State, I wanted to get their thoughts on being a craft distiller in the area. Many

BLACKDIRT DISTILLERY
IN PHOTO: JASON GRIZZANTI AND JEREMY KIDDE

of the challenges that newer distilleries are now weathering are ones that Black Dirt Distillery experienced many years ago with their cider.

Early on, Jason and Jeremy decided to include contract production as part of their business model. With that decision, space and storage became paramount to running a successful business. It is something that they believe every new distiller should consider when choosing their location and spirit. Much of our conversation revolved around the challenges that distillers in a more urban environment face, versus what distillers deal with in a more rural location.

"Choosing a spirit that requires less space, like vodka or gin, would make a distillery located in a metropolitan area more viable. Transporting spent grain, for example, is a natural part of the process and a real consideration. Factors like that can make costs really add up, plus moving big trucks through city streets can have its own challenges," said Jeremy.

Apple Brandy, Apple Jack, and Pear Brandy were some of the first spirits of Warwick Winery & Distillery that are now produced at Black Dirt Distillery.

When they transitioned to whiskey, it was due in large part to the change in law. As Jeremy expressed, "Our original distiller's license was before the farm distiller's license or A1 existed, because before the A1 and later the farm D license there was only the A license. That license cost $50,000 which was cost prohibitive for most businesses. Fifteen years ago, the market for craft whiskey was not as big as it is now, so that was a very daunting number. That cost did not include equipment. Now

you see the influx of craft distillers and the tremendous outlay of capital, and $50,000 no longer seems like that great an investment. But at the time, there was also more interest in supporting the larger brands, not craft. Back then, vodka was also more popular, and the renaissance in bourbon appreciation had not yet begun."

Their wines and cider sustained them during that period, and they did a lot of direct marketing throughout the years. Having their tasting room also exposed their brands to a large number of people on a regular basis. Those people had early access to their brandies and whiskeys, which created a lot of buzz around their whiskeys, especially. Many of the whiskeys were not even sampled, but were receiving a lot of buzz as they sat in barrels. The antici- pation was building just from word of

mouth. The emails and calls started to come in about its release.

As you can imagine, Black Dirt Distillery takes a lot of pride in their products, but they are very proud of their whiskey and bourbon. They want to create products representative of the grain. Their bourbon, for example, is made from 80% corn, allowing the character of the grain to completely come through. Just like their wines are made from fruit and are very fruit-for- ward, so are their spirits.

With regular corn, each kernel looks the same, making it easier to harvest and combine. Their corn is non-GMO, all local, and genetically diverse. Each kernel looks totally different, also translating to diversity in product, which is why they only use ingredients sourced directly from the Black Dirt region.

**Tastes and samples of the Black Dirt Bourbon and Black Dirt Apple Jack may be found at the Warwick Valley Winery's tasting room and store, located at 114 Little York Road in Warwick, NY 10990**

## THE ELEPHANT IN THE ROOM

(Compliments of Jorge Mendez, House Mixologist at Khe-Yo in New York, NY since 2013)
1 ounce rye (Rittenhouse / Bottled in Bond / 100 proof)
1 ounce apple brandy (Black Dirt / Bottled in Bond / 100 proof)
3/4 ounce sweet vermouth (Carpano Antica Formula)
1/4 ounce Green Chartreuse
1 dash Angostura Bitters
1 lemon twist

**Combinefresh ice (rocks). Serve in a double rocks glass and garnish with lemon twist.**

Black Dirt Distillery products can be purchased from the following locations:

Astor Wines & Spirits
399 Lafayette Street, New York, NY 10003

Warehouse Wines & Spirits
735 Broadway, New York, NY 10003

McAdam's Buy Rite
398 3rd Avenue, New York, NY 10016

Black Dirt Distillery products can be enjoyed at the following locations:

Dead Rabbit
30 Water Street, New York, NY 10004

Death & Co.
433 East 6th Street, New York, NY 10009

Nick & Toni's Café
100 West 67th Street, New York, NY 10023

## BLACK DIRT® MANHATTAN

2 ounces Black Dirt® Bourbon
1 ounce American Fruits Sour Cherry Cordial
1/2 ounce splash of Grand Marnier
2 dashes Angostura Bitters
1 cherry

**Combine fresh ice (rocks) & cherry. Serve in a double rocks glass.**

# HUDSON VALLEY DISTILLERS

Thomas Yozzo and Chris Moyer have been friends for 26 years. Over the years they often vacationed together with their families, and the topic of opening a business would invariably come up. As they discussed what they would do next in their lives, the ideas were many. They talked about everything from opening a campground, to having a golf course or a game lodge.

Tom used to make beer and wine as a hobby, and it occurred to them that distilling may be an idea worth considering. Chris, an avid researcher, began looking into the emerging craft distilling industry. After discovering the industry was growing rapidly, Chris realized it was something they could seriously consider. Being in law enforcement at the time, Thomas also began to notice the change in laws and how they were becoming more favorable to farm-style producers of spirits.

When they made the decision to move forward, in July 2013 they purchased a small farm and apple orchard in Clermont, New York. Hudson Valley Distillers opened for business in March 2014.

Tom and Chris very much pride themselves on sourcing all of their natural ingredients within a five-mile radius of their distillery, and creating local partnerships. The only ingredients that they are unable to get within that radius are their malted barley and some botanicals for their gin.

Their apple cider, rye, and barley are sourced from Migliorelli, a very successful local farmer. There is also a winery called Tousey Winery, which they source their pinot noir grape skins from for their Grappa. They also age their brandy in Tousey Winery's used port barrels. Recently they started a special project with a local brewer, Chatham Brewery, distilling their imperial stout from 80 gallons to 10 gallons, which they are also in the process of aging.

It takes them approximately one month, from start to finish, to create the majority of their products. However, their barrel-aged products range in time. Most everything that they do is single-barrel. They do not blend. They are using some barrels from a New York cooper, who only recently started making liquor barrels as a result of the increase in local craft distillers.

Their Spirits Grove Vodka is made exclusively from apple cider, yeast, and

DAVE ASHBY

distilled water. Tom and Chris believed that, since they had an orchard, it was more authentic to create an apple-based vodka. However, they were originally planning on making it from Blue Adirondack Potato, but hesitated due to the challenges often associated with potato starch. Sourcing was also not economically feasible.

After going through many different types of yeast, Tom and Chris settled on the one that imparted the flavor that they were looking for. Tom also cuts deep into the heart of their vodka, allowing only for a quality product.

DAVE ASHBY
IN PHOTO: CHRIS MOYER AND THOMAS YOZZO

Realizing the high demand for brown spirits, there is quite a bit of product barrel aging at Hudson Valley Distillers. Their Adirondack Applejack is made from Hudson Valley apples and aged in white oak. Their Hardscrabble Applejack has a strong American oak start, with hints of caramel, and vanilla. Their Chancellor's Raw Bourbon is named after one of Hudson Valley's great patriots and is a premium white whiskey made from corn and malted barley.

They were working on their Clear Mountain Gin and their whiskey, which are due to be released in 2015.

Tom and Chris want to be true to their goal of making their products different and unique. Their business model is to make their location a destination, with the addition of their cocktail lounge, Cocktail Grove.

ALL THE TASTES OF NEW YORK

**Hudson Valley Distillers' Products can be purchased from the following locations:**

Viscount Liquors
1173 U.S. 9, Wappingers Falls, NY 12590

Mid Valley Wine and Liquor
39 North Plank Road, Newburgh, NY 12550

Sipperly's Grogge Shop
7510 North Broadway, Red Hook, NY 12571

**Hudson Valley Distillers' Products can be enjoyed at the following locations:**

Culinary Institute of America
1946 Campus Drive, Hyde Park, NY 12538

Flat Iron Restaurant
7488 South Broadway, Red Hook, NY 12571

Renaissance New York Times Square Hotel
Two Times Square, 714 7th Avenue at West 48th Street, New York, NY 10036

## BASILBERRY BUZZ

1 1/2 ounces Spirits Grove Vodka
1-2 large fresh basil leaves
1/4 cup strawberries
Splash of simple syrup
1 ounce lemon juice
3-4 ounces chilled soda water

Basil is rumored to be an aphrodisiac. Rev up your life with this delicious basil- strawberry cocktail.

In shaker, muddle basil & strawberries, add ice, vodka, syrup, and lemon juice. Cap and shake. Pour into glass, add soda water and garnish with strawberry and basil leaf.

The distillery hours are Friday–Sunday 12 PM to 6 PM for tours, tastings, and bottle sales. Tours are at the top and bottom of the hour, or by appointment during the week.

Hudson Valley Distillers is located at Spirits Grove Farm, 1727 Route 9, Clermont, NY 12526

## NONNY ROSE

2 ounces Adirondack Applejack
1/2 ounce Grenadine (the real stuff)
1/2 ounce lemon juice
1 slice of lemon

A take on the Jack Rose, this cocktail is like Tom's great grandmother... a real classic, not too sweet, and packs a punch!

Stir the ingredients with ice and strain into a cocktail glass.

## HUDSON HIGHBALL

1 1/2 ounces Adirondack Applejack
Dash of orange juice
1/2 ounce ginger beer
Lemon slice

Traditionally made with whiskey, enjoy this classic with America's first spirit.

Combine ice, Adirondack Applejack, orange juice, and ginger beer. Garnish with lemon slice.

# JACK FROM BROOKLYN- SOREL

Jack Summers is the founder of Jack From Brooklyn, a company he created to produce the liqueur Sorel. Jack has been making the basic recipe for Sorel over 20 years in his kitchen, to be enjoyed by friends and family. It's a flavor that he grew up with. His grandparents were originally from Barbados, and they migrated to America in the 1920s. They brought the flavor of this drink that has its roots firmly planted in the Caribbean, with them.

In 2010, Jack had a cancer scare. His doctor found a golf-ball-sized tumor in his spine, and he was told initially that it was a fatal form of cancer. The tumor had to be removed and, fortunately, was benign. From that day, Jack felt like that experience was like dodging a bullet, which left him reassessing his priorities. He had already invested 25 years in corporate America and, although he had a job that made a lot of money, he was very unhappy. It seemed to make sense to spend the rest of his days doing something that mattered, with people he cared about and wanted to be around. As it turns out, he cares about alcohol.

Jack decided to take the beverage that he has been making in his kitchen for so many years and find a way to turn it into a commercial venture. As a person from the Caribbean, I was very curious to learn more about why of all the drinks native to the Caribbean, he choose sorrel. After all, it had been around for hundreds of years and is rarely seen outside of the Caribbean, and even less outside of West Indian communities.

As Jack expressed, "If you have an idea that you think is so good that no one has thought about before, it is probably a bad idea. Either that or no one has solved the logistics of why it has not been done yet."

There were a number of things that Jack was already doing in his kitchen. His Sorel was one of them. He believed that he could figure out the shelf-stable version of the product. He knew that even just having the idea was crazy, because he doesn't have a degree in food chemistry. Although he had no reason to believe that he could do it, he still went for it.

ALL THE TASTES OF NEW YORK

Sorel is made from Moroccan hibiscus, Brazilian clove, Nigerian ginger, Indonesian cassia, and nutmeg. It took months of experiments and failure. Although he had the basic recipe for the flavor, that version, like every other home version, oxidized after four to five days. He woke up every day for months and made a batch. He would then torture each bottle from the batch he produced. He would put one in a bottle, one on the fire escape, boil one, freeze one, nuke one, leave one in the back of a car, the other in the sun; anything he could think of to see if it would break down. For the first few months it was an exercise in failure, and he began to think that the reason that sorrel had not been commercialized before is because it could not be done. But failing over and over again didn't stop him. Eventually he found a version that was shelf-stable. It took him almost five months.

Once he achieved the shelf-stable version, he knew that he had a product he could work with. Twice he had to redo the recipe. The first shelf-stable version was made with spices that he purchased retail. However, once he increased production and had to transition to commercially-available spices, the potency was much greater. It took another month to perfect that recipe since it had to be reworked to balance the spices in proportion to each other. He also had to determine the best alcohol percentage, and how to create it on a larger scale and the correct ratios. Before that point he was still making it in his kitchen, two gallons at a time.

In the Caribbean, almost every drink is made from rum, since sugar cane grows abundantly and there are a number of rum distilleries. Although Sorel has Caribbean roots, the spirit used is a neutral wheat grain spirit, since rum has too much personality to lend itself well to a liqueur.

Six months after Jack opened for business, Hurricane Sandy came along in October 2012, and devastated Red Hook, the home of Sorel. Jack's entire establishment and everything in it was covered by six feet of water. Everything was destroyed. The product, equipment, and the distillery sustained infrastructure damage. With the help of friends and neighbors, Jack reopened in January 2013 and, by the end of 2013, Sorel was in 22 states, Canada and Australia and, appropriately so, in Trinidad and Tobago.

Sorel will mix with anything in a bar: gin, rum, vodka, mezcal, whiskey or scotch. The limits are only based upon each individual's imagination. It is a product as diverse as the founder himself.

Summer Lee, Jack's vice president, moved to New York City in June of 2012. In early October 2012, she went to a liquor store and heard Jack telling his story while doing a tasting. She was on her way to a party and decided to purchase a bottle of Sorel to take to the party. As the evening progressed, the bottle of Sorel was being passed around and was enjoyed by everyone. It occurred to her, being in the industry, that having such a large number of people receive a product so well is a rare experience. She took note.

Summer kept in touch with Jack and had the opportunity to get involved with the brand, starting as his general manager. She was responsible for promoting on-premise and off-premise and at different retailers. Now as the vice president of Sorel, Summer feels a sense of purpose since it is all very hands-on, and she has the ability to directly impact the business.

Sorrel has been in the Caribbean for 400 years, and had not gone mainstream till now.

Jack also has other products in the works. "How many other drinks are out there like that, waiting for someone to discover them?" Jack says about Sorel.

Jack's intention is to establish the brand and travel the world, seeking niche products, figuring out if they can be successfully and authentically created and produced commercially. The single qualifier is that the product has to speak to him. "Take something that is genuinely good but unknown because it is regional, and make it more mainstream," he said. There are few things in life more exciting than that!

## Sorel can be purchased at the following locations:

**Astor Wines & Spirits**
399 Lafayette Street (at East 4th Street), New York, NY 10003

**Gramercy Wine & Spirits**
104 East 23rd Street, New York, NY 10010

**Caroll Gardens Wines & Liquors**
427 Court Street, Brooklyn, NY 11231

## Sorel can be enjoyed at the following locations:

**DBGB Kitchen & Bar**
299 Bowery, New York, NY 10003

**Talde**
369 7th Avenue, Brooklyn, NY 11215

**Tavern on the Green**
Central Park West & West 67th Street, New York, NY 10023

## VERANO AMAR

(Compliments of Nicole Fey, General
Manager of The Vault inBoston, MA)
1/2 ounce Sorel
2 ounces tequila
1 ounce pineapple juice
1/2 ounce fresh lime juice
1 lime wedge
Cinnamon sugar

Rim a rocks glass with
cinnamon sugar. Combine
Sorel, tequila, pineapple
and lime juice. Shake with
ice. Pour into prepared
rocks glass. Garnish with
lime.

**Jack From
Brooklyn is
located at 177
Dwight Street,
Brooklyn, NY
11231**

## THE ARIANA

2 ounces Sorel
5 ounces Prosecco

Pour Prosecco into cham-
pagne flute. Finish with
Sorel.

Our signature summer
cocktail is named after
one of our favorite spirits
buyers. Perfect for lazy
Sunday brunches that
stretch late into the after-
noon/evening, the Ariana
is simple, beautiful, delicious, refreshing, and of
course, best enjoyed with
friends.

## SOREL SUBMERGE

2 cubes Sorel
2 ounces gin
1 ounce elderflower liqueur

Fill an ice cube tray with
Sorel, freeze. Place fro-
zen cubes of Sorel into
a highball glass. Add gin
and elderberry liqueur. As
Sorel ice cubes don't float,
they will sit at the bottom
of the glass, dissolving
slowly.

Enjoy a cocktail that is as
visually stunning as it is
delicious.

# COPPERSEA DISTILLING

Coppersea Distilling opened in 2012, and was founded by Angus MacDonald and Michael Kinstlick. A native of the Hudson Valley, Angus, their Master Distiller, had been studying the craft of fine spirit distillation for over 30 years. Michael, their CEO, who lives on the West Coast, brings entrepreneurial drive and acumen from over 20 years of business. Michael's prior work includes finance, software and commercial insurance.

Christopher Williams, who I had the pleasure of meeting, is also from the Hudson Valley and was brought on as their Chief Distiller. Having a background in brewing and distilling, Christopher welcomed the opportunity to be Coppersea's Chief Distiller, since he and Angus were of the same mindset as to the kind of distillery that they wanted to start: one that reinvigorated American Spirits' making, returning it to its traditional roots.

The intent was always to create a distillery employing very traditional methods, and one that used Hudson Valley grain to make whiskey and Hudson Valley fruit to make brandy. From the beginning, the idea was always to make the distillery very traditional and hands-on. The term 'handmade' is

used by a number of distilleries, but few truly exemplify the meaning. Coppersea truly does everything by hand, from malting the grain, to the end product of bottling and labeling. They also recently purchased a farm in New Paltz, where they are growing their own grain and planting their own pear orchard, with the desire of producing the majority of their grain.

With as much experience as Christopher has as a brewer, he thought that his disposition was better suited to distilling. He finds the process more interesting, since many of the same skills are involved. He wanted to create a distillery that allowed for idiosyncrasy and terroir. In brewing there is a lot more emphasis on strict control. If not, batches can easily get ruined. Though there are a lot of distilleries that run like breweries, with distilling, things do not have to happen in such a knowable way. The team at Coppersea wanted to create a distillery that allowed for a bit more chance to be involved. For example, they work with open wooden fermenters, because they want a little more ambient yeast to get into the mash. They want bacteria and other natural organisms to add their uniqueness and character.

When Christopher expressed this, I began to wonder how they maintain consistency in their products. In Christopher's opinion, "Consistency means to formalize things that have seemed to be successful. When we like something that has happened, we go back to our records. We try to keep meticulous records to determine what it is we did and what about it led to that particular effect. Consistency, however, is not our primary goal. If you lock something in so that it is easily repeatable, you miss the opportunity for something to be exceptional. As long as we are paying attention and doing the best job that we can do from mash to mash, it is very rare that we will create something that is not good. It's the idea of locking something in that is 'just good' that is inherently limiting. We do not want anything that is 'just good'."

The way in which Coppersea is built defies any kind of conventional training or knowledge that they could have received. The distillery that Christopher was previously with was very modern in its approach, having rigorous controls and much more modern equipment, methods, and techniques. By comparison, everything done at Coppersea is 100% natural. They do not add any industrial enzymes to their mash to do the conversion. Everything happens on its own diathetic power. They malt the grain themselves and they also use direct-fired stills, which is a huge differentiator.

No other distillery in the country is combining all of these traditional methods (growing grains, malting, open-top wood fermentation, and direct-fired stills) like Coppersea's 'Heritage Methods Distilling'. No one has

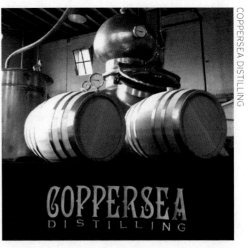

COPPERSEA DISTILLING

COPPERSEA DISTILLING

y

COPPERSEA
DISTILLING

really done it like this since 1890. When they asked an engineering firm to help them design a better enclosure for a direct-fired still, it was unheard of. They got most of their knowledge from potters, since potters were the only people in a trade who could relate to what they were talking about, since they were the only ones who had experience with direct fire and keeping the flame in an enclosed space.

Coppersea Distilling is located at 1592 U.S. 9W, West Park, NY 12493

Their first product, after trouble-shooting and coming up with a recipe, was an un-aged rye whiskey called Coppersea New York Raw Rye. It is made from 75% un-malted rye and 25% malted barley; 100% Hudson Valley Grain.

They made the Raw Rye because it is a historically-correct style. Although the reputation of un-aged whiskey is that it is a place-holder for distilleries--just something that they can sell--very often distillers put the same un-aged whiskey into a barrel and age it. Their Raw Rye Whiskey was never meant to be aged, since it is a historical style. Many people do not realize that, although un-aged whiskey appears to be a fad, in the 1890s, un-aged whiskey was the norm, and putting it in a barrel was just the way to transport it. As the country developed and moved westward, most of the whiskey distilling was still focused in the northeast--or generally on the east coast,

because of grain production.

It took longer and longer for spirits to get to the end user on the other side of the country, which is why aged whiskey is typically associated with the old west, because by the time it got there, it had been sitting in the hull of a boat, on a wagon or on a train, and was brown when it arrived. If you wanted whiskey, you had to drink it brown. There was no choice. The taste then re-migrated to the east, where people developed a taste for brown whiskey as well, though the whole process was very much by accident.

At Coppersea, they age 100% malted rye, bourbon, and brandy. They let the process communicate to them what the product should taste like. All that they do is make it, find the sweet spot, and reverse-engineer it. Doing so, they realized that their process is incredibly inefficient. As a result, the spirits that they get out of their stills are very broad in the flavors that they allow to come through.

Christopher told me, "Whiskey is an expression of where you are. We try to interfere as little as possible with letting the grain or fruit express its essential nature. We add as much as is reasonable to the evolution of the whiskey, as an expression of New York State and of the Hudson Valley."

ALL THE TASTES OF NEW YORK

## COLD TODDY

(Compliments of The Gander in New York, NY)
1 1/2 ounces Coppersea Raw Rye
3/4 ounce Amaro Montenegro
3/4 ounce lemon juice
3/4 ounce Earl Grey syrup (equal parts Earl Grey tea and honey)
2 dashes dandelion root bitters
2 dashes burdock root bitters

**Add all ingredients to a shaker. Add ice. Shake and strain into a coupe glass. Garnish with a lemon twist.**

## GANDER SMASH

(Compliments of The Gander in New York, NY)
2 ounces Coppersea Raw Rye
1/2 ripe peach
2 mint sprigs
1/2 ounce fresh lemon juice
Dash of peach bitters

**Muddle the peach, mint and lemon juice in a lowball glass. Add the Raw Rye and bitters, stir well and let rest for one minute. Cover with cracked ice and serve with mint garnish.**

**Coppersea Distilling products can be purchased from the following locations:**

Astor Wines & Spirits
399 Lafayette Street, New York, NY 10003

Stone Ridge Wine & Spirits
3853 Main Street, Stone Ridge, NY 12484

Acker, Merrill & Condit
160 West 72nd Street, New York, NY 10023

**Coppersea Distilling products can be enjoyed at the following locations:**

Fish and Game
13 South 3rd Street, Hudson, NY 12534

The Flatiron Room
37 West 26Th Street, New York, NY 10010

Peekamoose Restaurant
8373 State Route 28, Big Indian, NY 12410

## SEELBACH

1 ounce Coppersea New York Raw Rye
1/2 ounce Cointreau
3 dashes Peychauds and Angostura Bitters
Champagne orsparkling wine

**Stir ingredients together, strain into a flute and top with Champagne or sparkling wine.**

# BROTHERHOOD WINERY

**B**rotherhood Winery, located in Washingtonville, New York, produced its first documented vintage in 1839.

At the time of this writing, they just celebrated their 175th anniversary. I wanted to include Brotherhood in this writing because, with their very extensive history, they successfully weathered many of the storms that local distillers are currently facing. They have earned the distinction of being America's oldest and continuously-operating winery, also remaining open during Prohibition.

Acknowledging their location in the Hudson Valley, where a concentration of distilleries exist, Brotherhood also provides grape skin to local distillers to be used in the making of grappa.

With such an extensive history, there were many eras of families that made significant contributions to what has now become the legacy of Brotherhood. Winery founder, John Jacques, faced extensive challenges as a wine-maker for a public that wanted whiskey (1839-1886). Jesse M. Emerson and son, Edward R. Emerson, embraced the Industrial Revolution and modernized the winery to

bring it into the 20th century (1886-1920). Louis L. Farrell allowed the business to survive through Prohibition (1920-1947). Francis and Eloise Farrell, and daughter, Anne, pioneered wine tourism and history (1947-1987). Cesar Baeza was instrumental in Brotherhood being a producer of premium wines (1987-2005). The Castso-Chadwick-Baeza partnership has greatly modernized and expanded the winery into the diverse operation that it is today (2005-Present).

Before Mark Daigle arrived at Brotherhood, he was a teacher in California and worked his summers at wineries in Napa Valley. For Mark, wine started off as a hobby. After he stopped teaching, he decided to pursue the wine industry. He worked in the Burgundy and Champagne regions of France. He also spent time in Portugal and the Jerez region in southern Spain, all in an effort to educate himself about wine.

In 1976, as Mark was making the decision to return to France, a friend of his, who was the winemaker at Brotherhood and had started the position only three months before, invited him to stay for the crush. At the time, all of the equipment was French, which Mark was familiar with, so he agreed to stay.

Mark started off as the assistant wine-maker, and then became the head wine-maker. Through the years, he has seen many changes in Brotherhood and the New York Wine Industry. When the business changed hands in 1987, he went from being the head wine-maker to the production manager, and has been the production manager ever since. Brotherhood runs a very significant bottling operation, since they also do contract packaging. It is not uncommon to see a number of items bottled at Brotherhood in different stores under different labels.

Aside from their wines, Brotherhood's cider has become very popular. Their cider is a very American product. With apples being available year-round, they get the juice freshly pressed from their suppliers. Then it is fermented. When the apples ferment, they do so readily, and there are fewer challenges than the ones that often occur with grapes. On one hand, making hard apple cider is slightly less complicated than making grape wine, and fortunately the popularity has added to their business. Brotherhood makes cider for other companies as well, and in the last year they have added an additional 100,000 gallons of capacity.

With regard to maintaining consistency in products, and depending on the flavor profile that they are looking for, they source their apples accordingly, not unlike using a specific grape for a particular wine. There is a lot of trial and error involved. With the large number of people who visit their tasting rooms, they also allow them to try products that they are still perfecting. Encouraging participation is always good.

Over the years that Mark has been at Brotherhood, and especially being the production manager, he has experienced firsthand the challenges that exist going from an operation of literally a handful of people to one that employs approximately 70 employees. We began to discuss the challenges associated with businesses that make and sell as much as they produce without making enough to warrant greater distribution

to build their business.

Mark referred to this occurrence as the plateau system. "You can be very efficient and do a good job, be hands-on and have good business on a small scale. You're going to reach a certain point where things are going to leveloff, where you can't increase your volume or cash flow, even though you are selling everything that you make. You need to make a quantum leap. That means you need to get larger equipment. However, with larger equipment, now you are able to make more, but now you also have to be sure to sell everything that you produce. So, going from a couple employees and being craft, to having more employees will require a salesperson and a distributor to increase your footprint. It is all a very delicate balance. To make the quantum leap is very significant with all that is involved, with regard to licensing, distribution, personnel, and insurance, but it is all part of growing a business."

**Brotherhood Winery is located at 100 Brotherhood Plaza Drive, Washingtonville, NY 10992**

**Brotherhood Winery products can be purchased from the following locations:**

<u>Hamilton Discount Wine & Liquor</u>
3607 Broadway at 149 Street, New York, NY 10031

<u>Landmark Wine & Spirits</u>
7th Avenue, 23rd Street, New York, NY 10011

<u>Ambassador Wines & Spirits</u>
1020 2nd Avenue, New York, NY 10022

**Brotherhood Winery products can be enjoyed at the following locations:**

<u>A Casa Fox</u>
173 Orchard Street, New York, NY 10002

<u>The Old 76 House</u>
110 Main Street, Tappan, NY 10983

<u>Dopo East</u>
345 East 62nd Street, New York, NY 10065

BROTHERHOOD WINERY

# HILLROCK ESTATE DISTILLERY

**H**illrock Estate Distillery is the result of Jeffrey Baker's passion for farming, fine spirits, and the rich terroir and history of the Hudson Valley.

Jeff grew up in Western New York, working on farms. He moved to New York City in 1986, and realizing how much he missed life in the country, he bought a farm on the New York/ Vermont border within three years of having moved. Jeff raised one of the first rotationally-grazed dairy herds in the country, with the intention of making farmstead cheese. However, working as a banker in New York did not allow the

time necessary to dedicate to it.

Focused on value-added farming, Jeff later switched from dairy to beef, and had a 100-head Black Angus herd, which was also rotationally-grazed. Jeff

was one of the early advocates of the farm-to-table movement, and his Black Angus beef was served at his Saratoga Springs restaurant. His was one of the early grass-fed beef operations in this part of the country, before consumers were willing to pay a premium for grass-fed beef.

In 1999, Jeff and his family decided to move closer to New York City, and he purchased the farm that is currently the home of Hillrock Estate Distillery. He planned to start another value-added farming operation, but wanted this one to be truly special and unique.

While doing research on farming alternatives, Jeff discovered that the person who built their house in 1806 was a Revolutionary War captain. After the war, the captain became a very successful Hudson Valley grain merchant. This research became an inspiration for Jeff's endeavor, and it turned out that the captain also had a brother who lived about two miles away and owned the Hammer Town Scythe factory. It was the largest plant in New England that made equipment for cutting grain. Clearly, grain was a major crop for the region in the early 1800s, and Jeff began thinking about what products could be made with local grain.

In the 1800s, New York State grew roughly two-thirds of the barley for the entire country, and almost half the rye. The Hudson Valley was the country's breadbasket. Local

craft spirits flourished. Over 1,000 farm distilleries produced whiskey and gin, reflecting the unique terroir of the region. As time went on that changed. People migrated west as the soil became depleted. Then Prohibition forced the distilleries to close their doors in the 1920s.

With his farming background, Jeff knew that he wanted to be one of the world's few field-to-glass producers of fine whiskey. He didn't understand why distillers were not growing their own grain, much as a fine estate vineyard would grow grapes for their wines. As Jeff started to do research, Dave Pickerell's name kept coming up. Dave had just left Maker's Mark, where he had been Master Distiller for 14 years. He was writing articles about the potential for "terroir" in whiskey, and the fact that distillers had lost their connection to locally-grown grain, which creates unique characteristics specific to a region or field.

Jeff contacted Dave regarding an article he had written, and when Dave responded, a dialogue and friendship ensued. Jeff expressed his desire to start a farm-based Hudson Valley field-to-glass distillery. Dave loved the idea, and their partnership was born. Dave is Hillrock's Master Distiller, and is responsible for all aspects of production, from selection and growing of grains, formulating mash bills, distilling techniques, to selection of barrels, aging, and determining the final product. Jeff

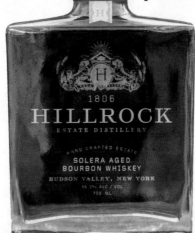

expressed, "Having someone with Dave's wealth of knowledge and experience as part of our team is critical in creating world-class whiskeys." Together with Tim Welly, their Head of Operations and Distiller, who was previously the Cellar Master at Millbrook Winery, Dave and Tim oversee the entire production process at the distillery.

Tim, Dave, and Jeff came up with the concept of Solera-aging their whiskey in 2010/2011 when they decided that they would set up the first Whiskey Solera in the United States. A Solera is typically used to age Sherries, ports and some Scotch whiskeys. Essentially a Solera refers to a pyramid of barrels, and new whiskey is put in the top barrels when it's made. The whiskey is older in each tier. You take older whiskey from the bottom tier, two to three times a year, and work your way down through the layers. The older whiskey essentially teaches the younger whiskey, modifying it and making it more complicated and interesting. Hillrock Distillery's Solera-Aged Bourbon Whiskey has won

a number of gold medals and Best of Class in many of the competitions that they've entered.

With a love of Scotch whiskey, Jeff determined that making world-class field-to-glass Scotch-style whiskey required building the first, new-purpose-built Malt House at a distillery, since before Prohibition. Floor-malting occurs in Hillrock's traditional on-site floor-malt house, where organically-grown estate barley is soaked and spread on a masonry floor to germinate. After several days of careful tending, the barley is then smoked and dried in their kiln and made ready for fermentation and distillation in their 250-gallon copper pot still. Brewers generally believe that the quality of the malt is superior when it has been traditionally floor-malted by hand, versus produced in a modern factory.

While local malt houses were once common throughout Europe and America, today only a handful of distilleries in Scotland still have traditional malt houses on-site. The vast majority of

IN PHOTO: JEFFREY BAKER - FOUNDER HILLROCK ESTATE DISTILLERY

HILLROCK ESTATE DISTILLERY

distillers worldwide now use "factory" malt, produced in bulk by several large corporations. Hillrock's Malt House provides the essential bridge between the estate's farming and craft distilling operations, and plays a critical role in the alchemy of turning local grain into fine whiskey.

In 2014, Hillrock harvested approximately 170 tons of organically-grown barley, rye, and corn. It was their first year of growing corn organically. Till then, they'd purchased corn grown by other local farmers, because these crops are very difficult on the soil. Everything else has been grown from day one from their own fields. They harvest and store their grain separately, crafting whiskeys from individual fields. As time goes on, the differences across fields will become evident in Hillrock's whiskeys.

Hillrock is committed to bringing back heirloom-grain varieties which are hardy, environmentally-friendly, and richer in flavor and complexity. They are also committed to sustainable farming methods. Their distiller's grain is used to feed local livestock after distillation. Tours and tastings are available by appointment by contacting Hillrock at 518-329-1023 or info@hillrockdistillery.com.

## HILLROCK ESTATE SOLERA-PEACH SMASH GRANITA

1/2 cup Hillrock Estate Solera-Aged Bourbon
2 cups water
3 ounces Perfect Puree White Peach
1 ounce simple syrup
1 teaspoon Perfect Puree Meyer Lemon

Combine all ingredients in a large bowl. Stir well to combine. Transfer mixture into a shallow pan and carefully place in freezer. After one hour, stir mixture with a fork. Stir again after 45 minutes, making sure to break up solid ice chunks with the tines of the fork. Stir every 30 minutes for the next three hours or until entire mixture is consistent icy flakes. Transfer Granita into freezer-safe, airtight container. Granita will keep in freezer for one to two weeks.

## STORM & SHADOW

(Compliments of Josh Rosenmeier of
Stockade Tavern in Kingston, NY)
1 1/2 ounces Solera-Aged Bourbon
1 ounce oloroso sherry
3/4 ounce fresh lemon juice
3/4 ounce blackberry cordial
½ ounce Demerara Simple Syrup
(Dissolve equal parts Demerara sugar and warm water. Allow to cool.)*
2 dashes orange bitters
1 dash absinthe
2 mint leaves
Mint leaves, fresh blackberries and
confectioner's (powdered) sugar for
garnish

Combine ingredients in
a shaker, fill with ice and
shake vigorously. Double
strain through shaker and
a tea strainer placed over
a Collins glass filled with
crushed ice. Garnish with
mint leaves, blackberries
and a dusting of powdered
sugar.

*Blackberry cordial: Com-
bine equal parts fresh
blackberries and white
sugar in a covered bowl
or Mason jar. Let stand at
room temperature over-
night, or until sugar completely dissolves. Strain
liquid and fortify with 1 to
2 ounces vodka. Will keep
in refrigerator, for three to
four weeks.

## PERFECT HUDSON VALLEY

2 ounces Hillrock Solera-Aged
Bourbon
1/2 ounce sweet vermouth
1/2 ounce dry vermouth
2 dashes Angostura Bitters
Maraschino cherry or small piece
lemon peel for garnish

In mixing glass or cocktail
shaker filled with ice, combine whiskey, vermouth,
and bitters. Stir well,
about 20 seconds, then
strain into cocktail glass.
Add cherry or twist lemon
peel directly over drink to
release essential oils and
serve.

# TIRADO DISTILLERY

**D**r. Renee Hernandez was inspired to create Tirado Distillery, the first distillery in the Bronx, after a visit to Puerto Rico in 2010. A tour of the Bacardi Distillery in San Juan was the pivotal moment for Dr. Hernandez, as he became intrigued by Bacardi's distillation process.

Having a background in organic chemistry from Fordham University, it occurred to him that he too could do this. The reason that he loved organic chemistry was because it allowed him to create things; and the idea of creating something new that deviated from what had already been done was very appealing.

Dr. Hernandez also had a number

of uncles who were moonshiners in the mountains of Puerto Rico, and had brought their craft to the United States. In his opinion, "The chemical part is very standard. What interests me is what it is that I am going to do to change the final product. How will I make it different? Distillation is very straight- forward, so now it's about controlling the elements. Once you control the system, it all becomes easier."

When he returned to New York, Dr. Hernandez started researching the law, which he realized had changed. He learned that as long as 75% of his ingredients were sourced from New York State farmers, he was able to qualify as a Farm D Distillery. Rum is distilled from sugar cane, which grows abundantly in the Caribbean. Since he lived in New York, he had to use something local, or else he would not qualify as a Farm D Distillery.

Dr. Hernandez realized that he could not distill rum, so he quickly began to experiment with whiskeys. Their next product was a clear whiskey that lends itself to many cocktails that would typically use vodka or rum. Tirado Distillery created this clear whiskey by distilling maple syrup. Dr. Hernandez then started experimenting with a fusion of the traditional Puerto Rican moonshining method with corn, and adding a bit of what they do in the mountains of Puerto Rico with the aging of their moonshine. By blending both cultures, he created a flavor that is distinctly Tirado.

Tirado uses organic corn from upstate New York and their mash is distilled and filtered twice through

HECTOR RODRIGUEZ JR

carbon filtration. They then age it in oak, until the flavor profile they are seeking is achieved.

Dr. Hernandez also uses corn and maple from local farms to create a corn whiskey, maple liquor, and rum. All of his ingredients are organic.

Their first product was a clear rum, named El Pitito. It comes from the family of El Pitorro. Pitorro, also known as Puerto Rican moonshine, generally has the reputation of having a higher proof. By calling this El Pitito, it implies that it is a lower-proof Pitorro.

Since their inspiration was fruit-infused rum, they wanted to treat their whiskey in the same way to create a whiskey that is easy to sip. They then created their dark rum, dark whiskey, and their maple liquor that is distilled and aged.

Given that Dr. Hernandez doesn't drink, I was very curious about how he settled on the flavor of what would represent his brand. "We did a number of experiments with wood, volume, and time, and had 500 to 1000 people taste the product to get an idea of what was more widely liked and well received," he told me. They have also recently started experimenting with French wood and are making adjustments in their aging process.

Tirado is now in its fourth year of production, and they are still very much a local boutique distillery. Most of their customers are throughout the Bronx and Manhattan and, as they grow the business, Tirado hopes to increase their reach to a much wider area.

## EL TIRADO

2 1/2 ounces of Tirado Gold
2 1/2 ounces of Goya Passion Fruit
Juice

**Serve chilled, without ice.**

**Tirado Distillery is located at 888 East 163 Street, Bronx, NY 10459**

Tirado Distillery Products can be purchased from the following locations:

St.Mark's Wine and Liquor
16 St. Marks Place, New York, NY 10003

Wine Stop NYC
30-8 Broadway, Astoria, NY 11106

Best Buy Wine Spirit Warehouse
701 Fulton Street, Brooklyn, NY 11217

Tirado Distillery Products can be enjoyed at the following locations:

Siete Ocho Siete
3363 East Tremont Avenue, Bronx, NY 10461

The Copper Still
151 2nd Avenue, New York, NY 10003

JP Restaurant
703 Minnieford Avenue, Bronx, NY 10464

## TIRADO VINTAGE MOJITO

Mint leaves
1 ounce of Tirado Gold
Juice from 2 limes
Club soda
Splash of cranberry juice
Sugar

**Shake and serve over ice.**

## TIRADO WHISKEY MARTINI

1 1/2 ounces of Tirado NY Corn
Whiskey
1 1/2 ounces of sweet vermouth
1 olive

**Shake and serve over ice.**

# TACONIC DISTILLERY

*formerly known as Millbrook Distillery

I met Paul Coughlin on a crisp December day, while he was bottling his second batch of bourbon at his farmhouse in Stanfordville, New York. Paul is the founder and driving force behind Millbrook Distillery. An avid outdoorsman and bourbon aficionado, Paul bought the property now known as Rolling Hills Farm, in 2010. Since Paul wanted to find a way to work the land, he initially looked into raising either sheep or cattle. However, he began looking into distilled spirits, as he became inspired by the corn fields and natural spring water on his property. They became the inspiration for Millbrook Distillery.

Gerald Valenti is Millbrook Distillery's co-founder. It was Paul and Gerry's interest in the outdoors and a simpler way of life that seeded the idea of Millbrook Distillery. Gerry is also a farmer, winemaker, and forager, and is instrumental in the selection of Hudson Valley grains utilized in their spirits.

A number of years ago, Paul was involved in a different venture that was looking into buying Maxim Magazine. One the things they researched was what could be done with the brand name. They had a number of ideas, and vodka began to resonate as a viable option. With Maxim already being an established brand, the idea of making vodka seemed like a natural progression. Quite a significant amount of time was spent determining how to make this happen and who they could make Maxim Vodka with, since it had to be outsourced. Although the idea never came to fruition, he very much enjoyed the process, and the idea of

ALL THE TASTES OF NEW YORK

distilling never left him.

In 2015, Millbrook will break ground to build a fully-operational distillery. The distillery will encompass a 5,000-squarefoot facility which will allow visitors to enjoy the tasting experience in addition to the distillery.

Millbrook is currently aging their bourbon and rye. The bourbon is aged a minimum of two years, and their rye is aged one year. As the business progresses, they will release more aged products.

Dutchess Private Reserve Straight Bourbon Whiskey has a bouquet of spice and honey with gentle notes of vanilla. It is a bourbon for sharing with friends.

Their Founder's Rye Whiskey is aged in virgin American white oak barrels, which adds a golden caramel color. It is bold with a spicy flavor and

a mildly sweet finish.

Limited Edition Barrel Strength Bourbon is bottled at 115-proof and is both bold and refreshing, with aromas of light vanilla, and hints of honey and caramel.

Previously, all of their bottling was done at their sister distillery, Still-TheOne Distillery in Westchester, New York, of which Paul is part owner. Once their facility is built, Millbrook will begin to distill all of the bourbon and rye produced from their 23-foot continuous-column still. They will also make use of their 115 acres of farmland to grow corn and rye.

Since Paul very much likes to drink bourbon and rye, he plans to position Millbrook Distillery as a lifestyle brand that creates premium aged spirits. In 2015, they will release a rum called Rolling Hills Rum, which is aged in bourbon barrels and finished in their rye barrels.

*"Millbrook Distillery has been renamed Taconic Distillery.*

**Millbrook Distillery products can be purchased from the following locations:**

Whiskey & Wine Off 69
1321 2nd Avenue, New York, NY 10021

Aries Wine & Spirits
128 West Post Road, White Plains, NY 10606

Empire State Cellars
308 Tanger Mall Drive, Riverhead, NY 11901

**Millbrook Distillery products can be enjoyed at the following locations:**

American Glory BBQ
342 Warren Street, Hudson, NY 12534

Culinary Institute of America
1946 Campus Road, Hyde Park, NY 12538

McKinney & Doyle
10 Charles Colman Blvd, Pawling, NY 12564

## WHISKEY SOUR

2 ounces Millbrook Distillery Dutchess Private Reserve
Juice of 1/2 lemon
1/2 teaspoon powdered sugar or
corn syrup
1 maraschino cherry
1/2 slice of lemon

Combine bourbon, lemon
juice, and sugar in cocktail
shaker. Fill with ice and
shake until frosty. Strain
into glass and garnish with
lemon and cherry.

## THE FOXHOUND

2 ounces Millbrook Bourbon
1 1/2 ounces sweet vermouth
1 1/2 ounces Campari
Orange slice as a garnish

Combine all ingredients in a
rocks glass and serve on ice.

## MAPLE-BOURBON SMASH

2 ounces Millbrook Distillery Dutchess Private Reserve
1/2 ounce pure maple syrup
1/2 ounce fresh orange juice
1/4 ounce fresh lemon juice
4 dashes Angostura Bitters
1/2 orange slice
1 1/2 ounces chilled seltzer

In a cocktail glass, com-
bine the maple syrup, or-
ange juice, lemon juice and
bitters. Add orange juice
and lightly muddle. Add
bourbon and stir well. Fill
glass with ice and top with
chilled seltzer.

*Carol Ann Coughlin is Millbrook Distillery's Chief Mix-
ologist and the creator of the following recipes. When
developing a recipe, she uses the tasting notes in the
spirit as her basis and layers them with fresh, seasonal
ingredients.*

# COOPERSTOWN DISTILLERY

Gene Marra was already a remarkably successful business owner, with over 40 years' experience as a chef and restauranteur, before he first arrived in Cooperstown, New York. He ended up there in 2008 for a restaurant consulting job. What developed for him in Cooperstown, however, was a passionate adventure into the world of New York State craft distilling, and the highly successful opening of Cooperstown's very first distillery.

Good restauranteurs become inevitably well-versed on the topic of alcoholic beverages, but Gene's enthusiasm ran deeper. Throughout his years of running his various restaurants, he had amassed a veritable wealth of knowledge, at one point even owning a vineyard and making wines himself. Gene had been experimenting with handcrafted gin and liqueur recipes in his own kitchens for years. His world-class palate and enthusiasm for intriguing flavor combinations, combined with his extensive business acumen, made things clear: he was ready to sink his teeth into a new challenge.

While living in Cooperstown, he learned that nearby Cornell University was offering courses in distillation, and he enrolled to deepen his knowledge of the distillation process. Taking one class on distilling affirmed what he already knew: he was on the right path. After a year of intensive schooling, opening a distillery had become his next big dream. Gene felt confident that his experience in the culinary world and his newly-found knowledge of spirit production would enable him to make a smooth transition into the distillery business. In 2011, he started amassing the necessary elements to accomplish his dream.

The Cooperstown Distillery officially opened on October 12th, 2013. But first, their still, the center of any distillery, had to be installed. Gene's still had been shipped all the way from Stuttgart, Germany, handcrafted by the finest still-makers in the world, The Carl family.

The initial test-run at the distillery after the still was installed was a huge success. The representative from the Carl family, Nicholas Haas, was extremely impressed with Gene's ability

# COOPERSTOWN
## DISTILLERY
### HANDCRAFTED ARTISANAL SPIRITS

to combine flavors, calling Gene's very first batch of gin one of the best gins he had ever tasted.

Gin is a neutral spirit, required by the FDA to only have one specific ingredient: juniper. Everything else, from citrus to coriander, to the more unusual botanicals, is up to the master distiller, which opens an enormous range of possibilities in the creation of intriguing gin recipes. Botanical-style gins, also known as New Western Gins, can showcase a distiller's ability, creativity, and talent, more so than with any other spirit. American gin distillers today are truly making products that are representative of themselves.

Following Gene's original recipe, the Cooperstown Distillery's Fenimore Gin is named after the prolific 19th-century American writer and Cooperstown son, James Fenimore Cooper, and features the flavor of native New York State lilac blossoms. Fenimore Gin includes the usual gin 'suspects' like juniper berry and citrus peel, but turns a corner with more esoteric botanicals like vanilla, mallow root, eucalyptus, and star anise. This 80-proof spirit awes the traditional gin drinker while making a more than a few converts!

Cooperstown is known throughout the world as the home of the Baseball Hall of Fame, and Gene wanted his brand to be deeply-rooted in the baseball culture of the town. Since its opening, the Cooperstown Distillery has swiftly expanded its offerings to

COOPERSTOWN DISTILLERY

include vodka, bourbon, whiskey, and rum. Naturally, baseball nostalgia has been a big influence in the naming of some of the distillery's creations, such as its BeanBall Bourbon, and Abner Doubleday's Double Play Vodka, which comes packaged in a patented, baseball-shaped bottle.

BeanBall Bourbon is a handcrafted blend of sourced Indiana bourbon and Cooperstown Distillery's own small batch bourbon, made with local corn, rye, wheat, and oats. Named after the dangerous baseball pitch, "the bean ball", thrown by frustrated pitchers to scare batters off the plate, Beanball Bourbon is incredibly smooth at 90-proof, with notes of caramel, butterscotch, and a sophisticated smoked toffee finish.

The Abner Doubleday Double Play "vodka in a baseball" is a stunning piece of baseball memorabilia. A wonderful tribute to the inventor of baseball, Abner Doubleday. This unique baseball-shaped glass decanter perches atop a ballfield-shaped pedestal. A perfect replica of an actual baseball right down to the 108 stitches, Doubleday's actual signature is etched onto every hand-blown bottle. It is filled with Cooperstown Distillery's 100% New York State, award-winning, white wheat vodka, which is distilled six times before being charcoal-filtered twice using a custom filtration process.

Its absence of a traditional vodka burn is remarkable. At 80-proof, this vodka drinks with a degree of softness that defies description.

The Cooperstown Distillery is fully-committed to honoring the legacy of their historical location, by creating products that pay homage to the rich literary and agricultural heritage of the area, while also indulging fans of America's favorite pastime. Aside from his still-growing passion for creating premium spirits, Gene Marra would feel honored if his brand became synonymous with memorializing the baseball in a bottle which, for him, would be a real home run.

REBECCA BERGFJORD

## COLD COCKED BEANBALL

1 ounce BeanBall Bourbon
1 ounce Fenimore Gin
1 ounce fresh lime juice
4 ounces chilled ginger ale
1 dash of Angostura Bitters

**Pour ingredients over ice, finishing with ginger ale.**

Cooperstown Distillery is located at 11 Railroad Ave., Cooperstown, NY 13326

Cooperstown Distillery Products can be purchased at the following locations:

Marketview Liquor
1100 Jefferson Road, Rochester, NY 14623

Warehouse
9 Halfmoon Crossing Boulevard, Clifton Park, NY 12065

Liquor Depot
739 New York 28, Oneonta, NY 13820

Cooperstown Distillery Products can be enjoyed at the following locations:

New York Yankee Steakhouse
7 West 51st Street, New York, NY 10020

Blue Mingo Grill
6098 State Route 80, Cooperstown, NY 13326

Otesaga Resort Hotel
60 Lake Street, Cooperstown, NY 13326

## FENIMORE FIZZ

2 ounces Fenimore Gin
1 ounce Barrow's Intense Ginger Liqueur
4 ounces Polar Dry Orange Soda
1 dash Fee's Cherry Bitters

**Combine gin and ginger liqueur and shake with ice. Strain, and pour over dry, orange soda. Dash with Fee's Cherry Bitters to finish.**

## WINTER ROGUE

2 ounces Glimmerglass Vodka
4 ounces freshly-squeezed clementine juice
2 ounces St. Germain Elderflower Liqueur
1 dash of your choice of bitters.

**Combine ingredients and shake with ice. Finish with a shot of soda water.**

# ACKNOWLEDGEMENTS

When I first conceived the idea to write this book, I had no idea how enriching the entire experience would be. I also did not anticipate that this project would accompany me to three different countries, one being my homeland of Grenada. As fate would have it, I had the privilege to get some writing done in the place that inspired me to start my business, South Beach, Florida. Admittedly, I did not make the best travel companion, but there have been many great stories to tell!

To my boyfriend, Amos, thank you for being so very patient and supportive during this time. You have made this all possible.

To my brother, Kevin, where do I begin? I am thankful every day that I am blessed to have a brother like you. I cannot imagine where I would be, were it not for the countless hours you have tirelessly dedicated to helping me build my brand over the years. From designing the cover of this book, to building my first website and everything in between, I am eternally grateful.

To my parents, for your constant support over the years, and my mother, who was with me at the very beginning.

To my brother Randy, as we embark upon this new chapter in our lives, thank you for sharing your tremendous knowledge that will steer the brand to a new era.

I am very fortunate to have many aunts and uncles who I am always able to call on at a moment's notice. Thank you for sharing your knowledge and advice.

To each distiller featured in this book, thank you for embracing this project and allowing me to tell your story.

To my publisher, Barbara, whose email introducing Waldorf Publishing changed my life; I never considered writing a book until that fateful day. Thank you for introducing me to a new and exciting world!

# AUTHOR BIO

## FOUNDER, ALL THE TASTES OF NEW YORK

**Heather D. Dolland is founder and owner of All The Tastes of New York, a startup firm that organizes and hosts themed "food crawl" experiential dining at some of Manhattan's top restaurants.** Launched in 2012, All the Tastes of New York enables groups of eight to 30 participants to enjoy appetizers, entree and desserts at three restaurants within walking distance of each other. Neighborhoods ranging from Hell's Kitchen and the East Village, to the Lower East Side, Murray Hill and Upper West Side. In addition, the company also provides brand promotion services to local wine and spirit companies.

"Food is the one language we all speak, and my goal is to curate experiences that propel dining from ordinary to extraordinary for my clients," says Heather, whose business has been featured on The Fox News Channel, New York 1, Queens Tribune, Times Ledger, SheKnows.com and Mike The Wine Guy.

**All the Tastes of New York** is the perfect venture for Heather, an accomplished amateur chef, and former Brand Ambassador for many premium wine and spirit companies. Her experience working with these brands and creating Food and Wine Festivals to promote them, led to her awareness of the increasing number of distillers in New York State. After getting to know many of these craft distillers, she was inspired to tell their story, in her book "Discovering The New York Craft Spirits Boom".

Today, Heather partners with more than 50 culturally diverse restaurants throughout Manhattan -from trendy neighborhood bistros to fine-dining establishments- to deliver an exciting culinary experience with exceptional service in memorable atmospheres. Heather's corporate clients include Match.com, Google, VeriFone, MetLife and Tumblr, and so far, 1,000+ guests have participated on the food crawls-an activity that lends itself to singles events, business outings and bachelor/bachelorette parties.

Born and raised in Grenada, Heather is a graduate of the American Sommelier Association and the French Culinary Institute. She is also working on becoming a Certified Specialist of Spirits.

Heather lives in the Murray Hill section of Manhattan. In her spare time, she enjoys traveling, cooking West Indian favorites of her youth and taking long walks in Central Park with her Schnoodle, Soca.

For more information, contact **Heather Dolland** at *www.allthetastesofnewyork.com*